With Love
To Grandpa from
Rick, Sue & Wayne
Christmas 198

"UPSIDE-DOWN" Pangborn

Photo courtesy of American Hall of Aviation History, Northrop University.

Clyde "Upside-Down" Pangborn.

"UPSIDE-DOWN" Pangborn

KING OF THE BARNSTORMERS

Carl M. Cleveland

AVIATION BOOK COMPANY
Glendale, California

Manufactured in the United States of America

Library of Congress Cataloging in Publication Data
Cleveland, Carl M 1903–
"Upside-down" Pangborn, King of the Barnstormers.
Includes index.
1. Pangborn, Clyde Edward, 1893 (ca.)–1958.
2. Aeronautics—United States—History. 3. Air pilots —United States—Biography. I. Title.
TL540.P29C57 629.13'092'4 [B] 78-12499
ISBN 0-911721-04-5

Design by Barbara Monahan

To H.M., M.J., and E.A.

Contents

Illustrations

Foreword

A NEW SPECIES of man ripped, roared and soared out of the cocoon of World War I. His swagger-type boots reflected the wings of his biplane; he spent $50 a pair for his tailored, flaring breeches and hankered after Army Air Service style shirts. His skintight helmet and his goggles, which gave him a devilish leer when lowered, were both his trademark and lady-bait.

He was the barnstormer.

His living was the sky—until sometimes he died.

He might wax his moustache to long points, install amulets to remove evil spirits from his cockpit and his wings, fly with bottle or jug to ease the hazards of his journey from rough take-off to rougher landing, ride a ship shining and clean, again a rachetic, sagging hulk.

Essentially, he was a pioneer throwing off the shackles of the ground as once the brave before him fired a gun at Brandywine, or got trapped in the northwest mountains, or tore from the stiff east to free west. He was blasphemous, profane, a knower of the best bootleggers from coast to coast, and physically alert to a female anxious to trade the comforts of a bed for a quick ride over town before he moved on to the next pickings.

Tramp? Philosopher? Pioneer? He was also an evangelist.

While he slammed America in the face with his aerial, he woke it to the need for air transportation.

He lived from January 23, 1919, when the government lifted restrictions on private flying, into the 1932 twilight, when time and his public climbed into cabined, multi-engine airplanes.

Interluding brawling, quick loving and faster death, he gyrated above the sunburned tonsils of half a nation. He introduced his sky to more millions of apprehensively adventurous citizens clutching tin-type cowlings.

His greatest creation was the Gates Flying Circus, which reached infancy in 1919, bawling lustiness in the twenties, and its end, under the name of The Flying Fleet, on a chilled, windswept field at Palo Alto in 1931.

Under the partners, Ivan R. Gates and Clyde "Upside-Down" Pangborn, this great organization—

Appeared in more than 500 cities.

Was the only integrated and personally owned barnstorming team to exist through many seasons.

Carried more than a half-million passengers.

Dedicated some 300 airports.

Cavorted above millions of startled beholders.

I'm just here opening the show so that you can, in the words of the ticket-sellers, fly with the birds and the bees—see your home town from the air with these death-defying devils, the world's greatest aviators.

Pangborn, who lived through the brawling, uncertain, quick dough, easy demise days, went on to do some amazing things after he retired as king of the barnstormers. He flew around the world, winning the Asahi Shimbun prize for being the first to span the Pacific non-stop with Hugh Herndon, Jr.

He placed third with Col. Roscoe Turner in the London-Melbourne race in 1934. He tested Burnelli planes built in the United States, Canada and England. As a senior captain in the RAF Ferry Command he delivered more than 150 aircraft across the oceans to the allies in England, Italy, Africa, India, Iran, Manila, Singapore and Australia. He made a half-dozen trips around the world and looked down from the skies on most of the earth's surfaces.

So here's Pangborn's story of the rollicking, wild, exciting, and at times incredible days of barnstorming and subsequent adventures.

LOWELL THOMAS

Preface

THAT MAJOR PORTION of this book dealing with the flying circus era (1919-1930) is based, to substantial degree, on a personal history maintained, but never published, by Clyde Pangborn. He compiled a complete and accurate running account of the barnstorming days of the 1920s, and of the unique breed of men who were the barnstormers. This material I have edited, rewritten and rearranged. Because he spoke the language of his barnstorming peers, much of his verbiage has been retained. To that extent, Clyde Pangborn might well be considered as co-author of this book.

During the barnstorming days Clyde scrupulously saved materials pertaining to his activities—letters, clippings, photos, accounting records, telegrams, posters, etc, all of which he sent to his mother for safe-keeping. On his death all this memorabilia was donated by his mother and his brother, Percy, to the Archives Division of the library at Washington State University, Pullman, Washington, where it is classified as The Pangborn Collection. The material fills some 40 standard reference file boxes. Dr. Earle Connette, librarian of the Archives Division, and his staff were most helpful in assisting my review of this collection.

In order to achieve as high a degree of accuracy as possible in regard to aeronautical references, the author has consulted various present and former personnel of The Boeing Company, Seattle, Washington, on technical and historic matters. Among those who have been of material assistance—some unknowingly—are Lysle A. Wood, Don Finley, N.D. Showalter, Gordon Williams, Lew Wallick,

William Worden, Tex Johnston, Harold Mansfield, Vern Manion, By Wingett, Elliott Merrill, Fred Collins, Clayton Scott, Amos Wood, Pete Bowers and the late Harl Brackin.

I am most deeply indebted to Percy Pangborn for his wholehearted cooperation in making available Clyde's written record of the circus days and allowing selection of pictures from his collection.

The sound criticism and valuable suggestions of John Underwood are reflected in numerous corrections made in the original manuscript.

A low and sweeping bow to Lowell Thomas whose foreword has so caught the spirit of the barnstormers who roamed the country in the 1920s.

It was in 1930 that, as a young newspaper reporter, I first met Pangborn. He had returned to Wenatchee, Washington, to visit his mother and brother. My first glimpse was typical of Pang—he was flying upside down the length of the town's main street.

Our last meeting was during World War II. He had come to Seattle to visit the Boeing plant and to demonstrate the Halifax bomber. I took him through the plant after which we sat in the cockpit of the Halifax and rehashed the Pacific flight, the dramatic ending of which I have covered in this book.

Clyde E. Pangborn was one of America's greatest fliers. I humbly hope that I have been able to project some of his extraordinary accomplishments in this book.

CARL M. CLEVELAND

"UPSIDE-DOWN" Pangborn

1

Drama Over Texas

SILHOUETTED AGAINST the blue of the Texas sky the slim girl, windlashed, swings pendulum-like beneath the airplane. Her rag-doll body twists and turns below the linen, wood and wire fuselage and a quarter-mile above a hundred-thousand gaping, apprehensive spectators.

Hers was to have been the climatic parachute jump of the day, a feature attraction of the Gates Flying Circus's "Thrilling Aerial Demonstrations."

Rosalie Gordon, once gay in a white silk jump suit, is "hung up." Her 'chute hasn't opened because, for some mysterious reason, her weight hasn't pulled it from its sack. So, after jumping from the cockpit, she is dangling at the end of 15 feet of rope tied to one of the wing struts.

At the controls of the plane is Clyde "Upside-down" Pangborn, half-owner and featured performer of the circus. He's the most scared man in the sky this February afternoon in 1924. Below, he sees Rosalie's closed eyes, her blue-white skin, her parted lips. He realizes that the hypodermic of fear has knocked her out.

She had come to the circus voluntarily; pleaded for the chance to make a jump at this Army Air Service sponsored show. Only yesterday, she had made a smooth rehearsal jump. Her eyes had filled with accomplishment after she landed. She's too young to realize that death is a real thing, therefore is willing to gamble against it in one quick roll.

Time is ticking, and Rosalie is the weight marking the ticks. She doesn't know the plane's fuel is running low. But Pang knows and so does Milton Girton in the front cockpit. Milton is a strong, flat-stomached young wing-walker-mechanic who stares over the side of the passenger cockpit. With puzzled, alarmed face, he looks back at the pilot.

"Grab rope," Pang shouts against the wind. "Pull!" Girton scrambles from the cockpit, grasps the rope and his body tightens under his flying jacket as he pulls. He straightens slowly, his face straining, his body twisting, taut as piano wire. A foot, two feet. A man against gravity, wind, friction—and dead weight.

"Give me rope you've pulled." Milt nods and Pangborn sticks out his left hand, gets a grip on the rope. Girton bends, strains, harvests a few more inches of rope and the slack is taken up. He bends again, gains a few inches, only to pant: "No go."

Pangborn knows this too. His hand has weakened. He senses the crowd below; the throbbing engine warns that time is short; the swinging body of Rosalie marks its winging. A bit of paper, a stubby pencil; Pang scribbles a note, pulls off his helmet, jams the note inside.

"Send up plane with Freddie and Tommy to make plane change." The helmet arches downward toward the other two red planes of the Flying Circus, bright in the sun of mid-afternoon.

Rosalie swings center stage in the damndest drama of her life. A crimson ship gathers speed across the soggy field. Tommy Thompson and Freddie Lund are on the way up. Thompson, flying the plane, is remindful of his fictional Texan prototype, the cowboy galloping across the plains to save fair maiden. Lund, a friend not even employed by the show, is in the front cockpit showing a large knife.

Thompson signals he will jockey below Rosalie, raise slowly until Lund can cut her free so she can drop into the cockpit with him.

"No! No!" Pangborn shakes his head violently. The swaying, swinging girl, being pushed sideways and backwards by the wind and then rocking forward, will go into their propeller; be chewed to death. Pangborn pulls away. Suddenly he is conscious that he is flying in a huge formation of planes; Army and civilian. Martin bombers, MB3s, SE5s, Standards, Orioles, Spads. Every plane from Ellington field is in the air. Everyone is trying to help—nobody can—and this is confusion.

Pangborn thinks he "feels" the Hisso cough. He motions agile, bowlegged Lund onto the left top wing of Thompson's plane where he can brace himself against the strut supporting the top wing overhang. Pangborn moves his ship in from behind, lays his right lower wing against Thompson's upper left, Lund steps across.

"You and Milt. Down on the landing gear. Try to pull her up," Pang directs. He is happy about that landing gear, if a man can be happy at this moment. It is a cage of wire, wood and metal. Front and rear, wood braces run down to axle and wheels. Wood fairings encase the axle, and to keep the wheels apart and in line a spreader bar. This entire structure, in turn, is braced by heavy cross wires running at all angles.

Minutes speed by. At the controls Pangborn can feel the movement of Lund and Girton on the bar. His palms are wet against the stick. He listens for the first sputter of the engine. He glances around at the helpless pilots and their helpless planes, faces grimly saying so far so good.

Lund comes up, his face close to the windshield. He is panting. The wind tears the words from his lips.

"No strength left. Milt and I hauled just inches."

"Slide under me. Fly the ship. I'll try."

Little Lund scrambles in, takes over the controls, while Pang lowers himself to the undercarriage and drapes himself around the right rear landing gear strut. With Milt he tugs at the rope and they gain a few inches. As he pulls, his weight is against his left cheek which is being sliced by the brace wires. He doesn't feel it, though it leaves scars which are to be with him the rest of his life.

A few inches. Hold—get breath. A few more inches. Hold. Inches gained; fewer inches lost. Inches make a foot, feet make a yard. Two yards, three, four. A yard to go! Then, as if cued, Rosalie shakes her head groggily just when she can help; when safety is in reach. Her eyes open. She struggles uncomprehending for a moment. Then she smiles wanly. Automatically the men on the spreader bar each lower a leg.

"Grab our feet!"

Uncertainly her hands come up. As she gathers strength she grips the boots. She is eased up, slowly, slowly. At last she is on the bar!

"Hold her—tight," Pangborn gasps as he drags himself through the wire and wood framework, back to the rear cockpit. There, with leaden arms, he takes over the controls, circles, eases back the throttle, and comes in.

As the wheels touch, a furious, joyous madness sweeps through the multitude who have watched the drama from the ground. They stampede toward the plane, running, pushing, shoving. The first eager, extended hands reach the side of the cockpit. Pangborn can't lift his arms to take them.

From what seems far in the distance comes the voice of Milt, still on the undercarriage, still clutching Rosalie.

"Stop that engine, you damned fool. Do you want to kill somebody?"

Aaron F. "Duke" Krantz, who had just joined the circus that day as a parachute jumper, solved the mystery of the nonopening 'chute. It had been packed the night before and had been left outside in the rain.

Rosalie Gordon and the men who rescued her after her parachute "hung up" beneath Pangborn's plane. Left to right: Freddy Lund, Pangborn, Tommy Thompson, and Milt Girton.

The new rope, around the mouth of the case, had shrunk. Krantz loosened it, went up and made his jump with Rosalie's 'chute.

There in Houston the saving of Rosalie Gordon was a momentous come-of-age birthday for the circus because it marked graduation from the small towns and the wheatfields to the larger cities of the nation and better airports.

The diploma was presented by the news services and the newsreels. It came in triplicate—the story of the dramatic episode pouring into the editorial rooms of the nation's newspapers, doubled by photographs, and tripled by newsreels rushed up and down and across the land.

Rosalie still wore her pretty white jump suit at the press conference.

"No, I wasn't afraid," she repeated to all questions. Later that evening she collapsed, was put to bed, where she stayed for the next twenty-four hours.

Following the press conference Ivan R. Gates, the tempestuous partner in the circus, confided to Pangborn that during the hang-up he had been racing wildly up and down the runway in his car.

"What good did that do?" Pang asked.

"I wanted to help."

Somehow, the circling of the military and civilian aircraft didn't seem so useless after that. They at least were up there in the sky.

Later, in the evening, Pangborn checked the fuel in his gas tank. Less than a pint remained.

2

Barnstorming Is Born

BARNSTORMING was a phenomenon of the post World War I years. Most passenger-carrying flights in that period were made from farmer's fields. The fields, in turn, were usually adjacent to the farm barn, which invariably was painted red. At some early period a nameless, but observant, farmer had exclaimed, "Here comes another of them barnstormers," as a plane made an exploratory buzz of his field. The term "barnstormers" is of earlier uncertain origin, but peculiarly descriptive of those post-war fliers. It caught on and became a part of the lexicon of aviation.

Following the 1918 armistice the price of a war-surplus plane varied from five thousand to an eventual low of three hundred dollars. More than 13,500 aircraft had been produced by the Aviation Manufacturing Association during the war. This glut of aircraft was to hold up design progress; prove a stumbling block to aviation progress for years. Yet scores of these planes were to fly from hundreds of farm fields, give the excitement of powered flight to thousands of passengers and thrill spectators with some of the wildest stunts ever conceived.

What of the great number of Army and Navy pilots who had been trained in the brief period 1917-1919? Never innoculated with the flying virus, the majority—pilots of varying skill—scurried back to their offices, stores, factories, garages, warehouses and farms. There they settled down, never again to touch a joy stick, as firmly earth-bound as the plodding animals of the field.

A few bought a surplus plane, made brief passes over small towns here and there, faced wind, hail and rain; found it not to their liking and finally gave up. The discolored skeletons of their tired craft could be found in barns, garages, backyards, and in open fields.

Others, a limited number, first milked their surrounding communities of passenger-hopping prospects then settled down on a sod field and became "fixed base operators." For most, it was a matter of waiting for business that never made it the mile or two out to their cow pastures while their airplanes deteriorated and their flimsy wooden hangars fell apart.

There were exceptions, of course, but very few. They were the vibrant, hungry and, some said, visionary men who were to write their names in virgin skies for the next decade. Among them were:

George Haldeman and Roger Q. Williams, who gained fame in the "distance" flying craze of the late '20s. Ormer Locklear, Skeeter Elliott and Shirley Short, who blazed their way across silent films in Hollywood. Up and down the west coast roamed John B. (Tex) Rankin of rosy cheek and perpetual air-hunger; Frank (Spook) Clark and his chawed cigar butt; Howard Batt, Jerry Phillips and Vance Breese, who became a famous test pilot.

Ray Chalk moved into Miami and stayed for two generations; Curly Burns ranged from air show to air show in the southeast; Chet Clark and others gathered their wings at the Marina and on Crissy Field in San Francisco. Beeler Blevins blanketed the area around Atlanta. Eddie Stinson, from Jackson, Mississippi, designed, pioneered and tested, and finally died in a crash in the midwest. His sisters, Katherine and Marjorie, were among the first aviatrixes, as they were called, in the nation.

There were others: E.W. (Pop) Cleveland, aircraft firm executive who couldn't stay put and free-wheeled until his death in a rock-lined cloud over the Cascade mountains near Seattle; Red Mosier, an early mid-west operator who later became a vice-president of American Air Lines; Art Hanford, who founded an airline bearing his name; Clarence D. Chamberlain, who flew the junk dealer Levine to Germany; Eddie Hubbard, an early associate of William E. Boeing in the

Northwest; and Roscoe Turner, speed king of the late '20s and early '30s.

And then there was Clyde E. Pangborn, a youth from the mountain valleys of Idaho, who joined with Ivan R. Gates to create the greatest barnstorming flying circus in the nation. The two were absolute opposites. Socially they had nothing in common. Their business clashes were frequent. Yet in the ten years of its phenomenal existence the Gates Flying Circus carried more passengers, dedicated more airfields, staged more night-flying fireworks exhibitions and covered more territory than the next several circuses combined.

It was quite fitting, and perhaps natural, that fire should have brought Pangborn and Gates together, just as in logical sequence ashes were to mark their ultimate separation. In late 1921 Pangborn, who had been barnstorming for some two years since his discharge from the Aviation Section of the Army Signal Corps, had parked his Jenny on a field at Ashland, Oregon. First, he had carefully burned off the horsetails, grass and weeds from the area where he intended to tie down. This was standard procedure so that a carelessly tossed match or cigarette would not start a ground fire and thus destroy the single asset of the barnstorming pilot.

The next morning Pangborn looked out his hotel window, across the open spaces to where his Jenny should have been. No plane. He dashed to the field.

The Jenny was there, quite whole, but moved outside the circle he had burned. A stranger was leaning on the wing. He extended his hand.

"I'm Van Gates," he said. "Sorry I had to move your Jenny, but I have a Martin TT coming in."

They shook hands. Pangborn noted that the hand was soft, the nails recently manicured. Not the hand of a man who ground valves, spliced broken spars and greased rocker arms.

"Nice to know you Pangborn. I've been hearing about you. I'm a pilot too."

The derby hat was a bit incongruous with the breeches of cavalry twill and the well-polished Cordovan boots.

As the two men paced the field, they talked about aviation, its past and its future. Rather, Gates talked and Pangborn listened.

Gates modestly explained that he had been an auto racer. Then in the early days, when he had first learned to fly, he said he had been

Only photo ever made of Gates and Pangborn together. It was taken in 1926.

associated with Didier Masson, Louis Paulhan, Hamilton and Hoxsey, all famed pilots of their era. He asserted that he had flown a criminal in handcuffs from San Bernardino to justice in San Francisco. He claimed earlier marriage with a noted diva. He unblushingly averred that, as a press agent, he was better than Bill Pickens, the noted newsman who had exploited Lincoln Beachey to national fame. All this he related with a straight face as though he expected Pangborn to believe it. Why not? Many did.

Years later, in a moment of candor, Gates confessed to Pangborn that the only time he ever "flew" a plane was during the early days in Richmond, California. He said that he had gotten somebody to crank up a Burgess while he sat at the controls; that the throttle was wide open and the plane lurched forward and hopped a fence. The engine quit at that point and the plane plopped down after traveling about 100 feet.

"It scared the hell out of me," Gates admitted.

After their casual conversation in Ashland the two went their separate ways. Within the year they were to join in creating the most successful flying circus operation of all time.

3

A Vow to Fly

A FRECKLE-FACED, pudgy school boy, Clyde Pangborn, and his friend Swank had gone to the city ball park in St. Maries, Idaho, where it had been advertised the daring aviator, Paul Beck, would demonstrate that man could actually fly. His plane was a kite-like Curtiss pusher. The pilot sat precariously on a small seat, well ahead of the wings, fully exposed to the wind.

Beck's advance man, megaphone in hand, was telling the assembled townspeople: ". . . and furthermore, the aviator Mr. Beck, will not only fly, but will pay one hundred dollars to any resident of St. Maries who will dare to go aloft into the skies with him!"

Clyde dropped the ball with which he and Swank had been playing catch at the edge of the crowd. He raced, heart-pounding, up to the announcer.

"Mister! Mister! I'll fly. I'll ride with Mr. Beck for nothing. I'll . . ."

The announcer roughly pushed the lad aside.

"Beat it, you little bastard! Beat it! You're crabbing my act!"

Disappointed, hurt, but still thrilled by sight of the soaring airplane in its wobbly flight over the city, the two boys had crawled into their very secret small cave near their home. It was a place for serious discussions and day-dream plans.

"When I grow up I'm going to be an aviator like Arch Hoxsey, or Louis Paulhan, or Bleriot!"

"I'll fly before you will" Swank challenged.

"Bet you won't! Tell you what, Swank. We'll pledge ourselves and carve the date right here in this cave to remember it by."

They cut the date into the clay wall, shook hands and closed the small hole in the hillside. Swank was to remain earth-bound. Clyde seemed from birth to have been destined for the sky.

Steady nerves, self-control, confidence, a respect for fear, mechanical sense; these were, and are, among the attributes of the flier. From his earliest days young Pangborn gave evidence of these qualities.

When he was but three years old his mother had left him briefly in their fourth-floor Seattle apartment. The child was fascinated by the open front window. He pulled himself up on the sill. This was fun. Nobody had told him about gravity. He stood on the window ledge; strutted back and forth. A crowd collected in the street. Pleased with the attention he waved a small hand at the upturned faces. His mother, returning from her errand, followed the stares of the crowd. She raced to the apartment and quietly, so as not to startle him, whisked the lad from the precarious ledge. Clyde Pangborn had put on his first "wing-walking" show.

Clyde's mother and father both came west in covered wagons. The mother almost didn't make it because she was in a washtub. Her mother, Clyde's Grandma Lamb, had six little Lambs to round up each morning as the wagon train got under way from its night camp. One morning she overlooked the washtub and it was left at the camp site.

A few hours later another wagon train crept by in the dust.

"Hey! There's a washtub, and we could use one," someone shouted.

A man halted the willing oxen and went to retrieve the tub.

"Hell," he shouted, "there's a kid asleep in it."

The tub and its cargo eventually caught up with the Lamb wagon train. In the Lamb party was a young lad, Max Pangborn. He and Opal Lamb were eventually married and moved to a remote ranch on the Columbia River. There Clyde was born only a few miles from where that mile-long monolith, the Grand Goulee Dam, now checks the river in its flow to the Pacific.

Ever restless, Max moved the family upstream to another ranch.

A sparse living, cold winters, hot summers, loneliness—the travails of pioneering engendered in Opal Pangborn fortitude, stoicism, cool nerve and quiet reserve. These attributes she passed on to her two sons.

When Clyde was two his father and mother separated. Clyde went to live with his mother; his older brother, Percy, to live with his father. For a period Clyde's mother was married to Louis A. Jahnke, a boxer, professional ice skater, Alaska dog team driver, gambler and saloon keeper. Clyde grew up in the brawling life of Orofino, Idaho, where Jahnke ran a saloon. The smell of whiskey, the cloying odor of the lumber jack's damp boots, the weekly brawls—as certain as Saturday came around—combined to create a strong aversion to drink in any form in the young lad. Clyde was in his '30s before he took his first taste of liquor.

On occasion Percy would come to visit his mother and younger brother. During one of these visits the two boys somehow obtained "threefers;" long, thin, and very strong cigars which were three for a nickel. They proceeded to smoke the three in rapid succession. Their subsequent stomach unheavels cured them forever of any taste for tobacco.

At 14 Clyde's fat had disappeared along with the freckles. When other youths his age were looking forward to exchanging their BB guns for "22s," Clyde was carrying a 30-30 rifle and had been deputized to help capture a man wanted for murder. The suspect had holed up in a remote cabin on the St. Joe river. The sheriff said to young Pangborn:

"Clyde, I'm deputizing you because I know you're a good shot. I want you to come up and cover me while I flush this fellow out of his cabin. If he comes out with a gun in his hands and starts to raise it toward me, you shoot him."

Fortunately for the wanted man, he came out without a gun and with his hands up.

"I'd have shot him if he had threatened the sheriff," Clyde said. "He already had killed one man, one of the local loggers."

A few years later, having finished high school with honors both as a student and athlete, Clyde had a job tending flume on a logging operation, his dream of flying seemingly more remote than the roadless mountain valley where he worked. It was his responsibility to check for leaks, breaks, and jams along three miles of wooden trough down which flowed water carrying logs from the holding pond above. The water and logs moved along at ten or fifteen miles an hour and Clyde often rode them—down to a point. There the flume turned and plunged steeply some two hundred yards to the loading pond. For a long time cautious fear had made him hesitate to make the turn.

This day, however, he had made up his mind to go around the blind corner and down the mile-a-minute chute. It should be fun. There was a hazzard to consider; as he started the turn he would not know if there was a log jam ahead. He dug in his peavey and calk boots. The acceleration was so violent that the peavey pulled from the log and he discarded it. Down he went with a shout of exhilaration. The men below looked up, startled. Fortunately the steep flume was clear of logs. He rode free into the lower pond, smashed into it, was submerged to the waist. His spikes held, the log bobbed to the surface and he stepped to the bank.

A motion picture company happened to be photographing logging operations at the pond. The director came over. So did Charlie Gregory, boss of the logging outfit.

"Kid, can you do that again?" the director asked.

"Yes sir. That is, I think so."

"I'll give you twenty-five dollars."

"You won't give him a goddamn thing!" Gregory exploded.

He turned to the log buckaroo.

"Clyde, if you ever try anything like that again, I'll break your neck before you do it yourself. Now get back up that flume where you belong."

The future flier at least had demonstrated his sense of balance and a degree of cautious nerve.

By extension courses from the University of Idaho, Pangborn studied civil engineering and on the strength of these studies obtained a job with the Bunker Hill and Sullivan Mining Company, the noted lead-zinc-silver producer, at Kellogg, Idaho. The company had contracted for a new 200-foot chimney for its smelter; the contractor to be paid when it was determined that the stipulated height had been reached. Slide rules and triangulation failed to agree on the height of the finished job.

"Hell, there's only one way to measure that stack," Pangborn, the very junior engineer, declared. "Give me a chain and I'll go to the top and drop it down inside."

He attacked the embedded rungs, his aching arms protesting this challenge to their strength. Finally he reached the top. He stood on the rim and dropped the chain, showing that the chimney was exactly two hundred feet, seven and one-eighth inches in height.

"I'll go a lot higher than that when I fly," he promised himself in single-minded determination.

For years, in the Idaho forests, Pangborn had reached from the mountains, through the trees, for the blue sky beyond. He had watched the clouds as they drifted across the valleys and spoke briefly to mountain peaks. He soared with great-winged hawks as they rode the summer thermals. Some day he, too, would look down, rather than up.

Then, in 1917, colossal misjudgment by the German hierarchy brought the United States into World War I. The Aviation Section of the Army Signal Corps sent out a call for volunteers. The call reached even into the backwoods of Idaho. Here at last was that chance to fly. The promise, carved years ago in the walls of a small cave, would be fulfilled.

4

Jenny

AT EBERTS FIELD, Lonoke, Arkansas, Pangborn met his first true love—a Curtiss JN4D, commonly called a "Jenny." Large numbers of the JN4D were produced during World War I, strictly for training purposes. The Jenny was a biplane with spruce spars and ribs, linen covered. A maze of bracing wires created a veritable bird cage between the wings. An 0X5 engine, of 90 horsepower, turned a wooden propeller. The only instruments in the cockpit were an altimeter, an oil pressure gauge and a tachometer. The Jenny had an air speed of 70 to 80 miles an hour; it landed at 35 to 40. It was intended to convince earthlings that they could indeed fly like the birds.

To the youth who had maintained a one-track conviction that he would fly some day, the Jenny was a svelte beauty; a Loreli who would introduce him to the mysteries of the sky.

After eight hours of sloppy take-offs, wobbly flight and bouncing landings—learning the hard way—the instructor, Lieutenant Max Miller, had climbed from the cockpit.

"It's yours, Clyde," he said.

Alone in an airplane for the first time! Without the assurance of the lieutenant visible ahead he must take this machine into the air, fly it around the field, bring it to earth again. He was too busy to feel any thrill. He pushed the throttle, took off and circled the field at the prescribed altitude, turned and landed. Lt. Miller motioned him back into the air. More circles. Finally Miller waved him to the parking tarmac.

"Nice going, kid," he said. "Nice going."

John W. Underwood photo collection.

Curtiss JN4D, commonly called a "Jenny."

Pangborn thought back to those hard days in the Northwest, the ground school at the University of California, basic training at Dallas; the long months of heat, sweat, yearning for flight, He found it hard to believe he had been in the air alone. He wondered how he could get word to Swank.

After Eberts, there was a succession of training bases. Camp Dick, Love and Ellington fields, all dreary, dusty or muddy according to the season. Still in the United States when the armistice came, Pangborn looked back on several highlights that had marked his brief military career.

First, he had learned about the "deadly tailspin." There had been vague reference to this certain introduction to death, but the instructors, who had little more experience than their students, hadn't talked too much on the subject.

"If anything . . . well, funny . . . happens while you're flying, reverse the controls, kid. Just reverse the controls."

Assigned to practice, Pangborn was doing figure eights, making left and right banked turns around pylons and crossing over a central point between them. Bored, he steepened his bank, and he found his pants being pressed hard by the seat. Suddenly the airplane started acting up. Below, the hangars, the barracks, the field—the flat world he had known for months—all were speeding in a circle around him.

If he could have looked up from the ground he would have seen that the plane was in a near vertical dive and that it was spinning around its own axis.

He remembered the instructor's laconic advice. He put his head down inside the cockpit; stared at his feet. The stick was back. He reversed it by pushing it forward. Almost full right rudder. He shoved it full left. The mad whirling turned into a power dive. Hell, he had overlooked the throttle. He pulled it back. The Jenny leveled. The ground was 200 feet below.

The "deadly tailspin" had lost its sting forever; had become a useful tool for losing altitude rapidly, and a certain crowd pleaser.

From Lieutenant Albert W. Newson, Pangborn learned a maneuver which was to give him a nom-de-air and become his trademark. One day the lieutenant asked him if he would like to fly upside down, a technique introduced by the frenchman, Pegoud.

Newson demonstrated by slow-rolling the plane on to its back. They rode in a long glide, their heads to the ground, their bodies suspended against the safety belts. Seemingly they were looking up at the ground. Soon Pangborn was trying the maneuver himself and before long he was known around Ellington as that "upside-down guy." In a few months he became "Upside-Down Pang."

Loops were easy. He said to himself, "If you push the nose down and aim at the field, pull the stick back when you have enough speed, look at clouds and sky and then see the field again, you've done a loop." Spins, loops, upside-down flight; he practiced them until he could perform each without thought.

As the armistice came and peace settled over a badly scarred world, Pangborn and his side kick, Ralph Reed, were restless with the dull routine of flying by the book. They sought a safety valve, and found it in plane No. 314.

Pangborn started it by saying: "You know, No. 314 could be another plane if we had some water paint."

"You've got something there," Reed replied. "It could be 814, or 344, or 844, none of which is on this field."

With 314 thus camouflaged they dived on trains, flew down to Galveston and chased small fishing boats at water level, frightened farmers from hay stacks and investigated female sunbathers. They never were caught.

Ordered to Love Field, Pangborn saw there his first Jenny with a Hispano-Suiza engine which doubled the horsepower of the Jenny he had trained in. He also saw, and was impressed by, the DH4 DeHavilland with the huge 12-cylinder 400-horsepower Liberty engine.

There, too, he met the man who whetted the natural mechanical skills he possessed. Sergeant Francine, a Frenchman, adopted several of the young fliers into a private class. He taught them *why* an airplane flies, and how to mend it when it suffered ills. He taught them rigging, balance, wash-in, wash-out, torque, engine and airframe repair and a hundred more tricks of the good mechanic. He advised them that an airplane was not a machine of death, but something to enjoy, like a drink before dinner, a pipe after, or a stroll in the woods with the sunshine filtered through restless leaves.

The biplane lazing along at one thousand feet over the Sacramento delta was a used Jenny, unpainted, doped to tan translucence and still carrying the Army stars. It was the ninth plane to be sold to a civilian under the Wilson Act following World War I.

Pangborn was alone in the air, feeling the thrill of first flight in his own plane. He was exhilarated by the wind as it stung his face, and by the metronome beat of the rocker arms of the 0X5 engine up ahead. Now he could fly anywhere he liked, any time he liked, and make money from the thousands and thousands, everywhere, who wanted the excitement of a bird's eye view of the ground. He was no longer regimented, forced to fly around a field or make a cross-country hop knowing that he could only go to a designated target and then must fly back direct to his base.

Now he could challenge the clouds and the wind. He could soar around the great cumulus clouds that gather above the western mountains, lie in the shade of the wing, and seek to penetrate the blue of the sky. He could witness the sharpness of daybreak, sense the peace of dusk, smell the dewey freshness of a thousand fields, look beyond mountain after mountain, push back the horizon!

This was the flying he had dreamed of and waited for during the agonizing years when the goal seemed so remote. Yet, had you asked him exactly why he wanted to fly his answer would have been as vague as Leigh-Mallory's "because it's there." Which really was no answer at all, only a way of dismissing an impossible question.

Why had men crossed the oceans, pushed westward across the North American continent, or trekked northward through the African Veldt? What brought Pangborn's ancestors to America from Scotland, Ireland and England; Grandpa Lamb to Idaho in a covered wagon, or caused Clyde's father to move to a remote ranch on the Columbia River? Why has man looked upward to the skies, gained the moon, and even now prepares to probe the infinity of space?

Is it ego? Challenge? Restlessness? The desire for recognition? The self-satisfaction of accomplishment?

Pangborn would have been mute to any of these suggestions. He only knew that he wanted to fly, that he felt an enveloping peace when he was in the air, that the staccato exhaust of an 0X5 was orchestral to his ears, that the sensation of a loop—of flying upside down—was as intoxicating as the wine which he shunned.

The Jenny which Pangborn was flying north to a rendevous with Reed in Sacramento had been purchased for $5,500. The money, miraculously, had been loaned to him by the directors of the bank in his hometown. Possibly it was by way of marking winning of the war; maybe the country bankers saw a future in the sky.

Or perhaps they were impressed by the confident young first lieutenant with all of 100 hours in his flight log who had come to the nearby metropolis of Spokane, Washington and signed on as pilot with Northwest Aircraft Corporation. The corporation was R.C. McClellan, already a veteran airman and builder of exhibition aircraft.

His latest creation was a knock-down, single-place biplane with an 0X2 water-cooled engine. The radiator had been used previously by the famed Silas (Cy) Christofferson. The entire craft could be taken apart for easy shipment from one small town to another.

McClellan was still not aware that airplanes were being converted and new ones designed to carry people. He saw an airplane only

Just out of the Army in 1919, young Pangborn signed on as demonstration pilot for this airplane designed and built by R. C. McClellan (far left) of Spokane, Washington. The airplane could be taken apart and crated for shipment from town to town.

as something to startle a skeptical public. To this end he had contracted for a series of exhibition flights in the Spokane area. One of these took the inventor, his plane, and his newly-signed pilot to the latter's hometown, St. Maries.

"Hi, Mom," Clyde greeted his mother.

"Hello, Clyde," she replied to the son who had been away in the Army for more than two years. That was the whole greeting. Space was so infinite in the Northwest that one didn't clutter up the woods with words. People felt and sensed things rather than voicing them. Mother and son had always been like that.

A.B. Annis, druggist and a director of the local bank, was among the crowd which witnessed Pangborn's exhibition flight, including the tail spin and loop.

Later, walking down the main street with Annis, Pangborn said:

"I'd sure like to have a Hisso-Jenny. If I owned an airplane like that, I could carry passengers as well as do exhibition flying. I'd make a million . . . "

"Why not?" Annis asked.

"A thousand reasons. The first one is no dough."

"Then let's go to the bank. I think we can arrange a loan."

With six thousand dollars, more money than he had ever had in his life, Pangborn took the train east to Lincoln, Nebraska. He had heard that the Curtiss Company there was selling airplanes. Curtiss airplanes. Jennys.

He found the company in a small warehouse.

"There must be some mistake," the lady said. "We don't sell airplanes. We sell magazines. We represent the Curtis Publishing Company. You know, *The Saturday Evening Post* and *The Country Gentleman*. Now if you'd like to subscribe . . . "

Eventually he found his Jenny in Southern California. When he and Reed met in Sacramento they decided to work up and down the coast—barnstorming it was called—carrying passengers on short hops at $10.00 a ride. Their method of calling attention to their presence in a community was sure-fire. They made wild, low passes over the small agricultural and cow towns; looped, spun, rolled and then went back to the field they had rented to await the crowd which always came. Six hundred dollars in three days at the small town of Montague, California; $50.00 to fly Claude Gillis, Yreka banker, to Medford, Oregon—the first interstate passenger west of the Rockies; $500.00 at Roseburg.

Gravy! But troubles too. Broken propellers, fractured wing spars, torn fuselage fabric and bent landing gear. For a new propeller you wired the Jacuzzi brothers in San Francisco. The repairs you made yourself.

Taking off at The Dalles, Oregon, to keep a July 4 date in Pang's hometown, Pang and Reed both had their eyes on a high post to their right. Neither saw the heavy bushes to the left. A lower wing hooked them and the airplane spun around, coming to a stop facing the opposite direction. The propeller was smashed, the landing gear torn off.

"Considering the terrain and the condition of our airplane," Pang said, "let's ship it."

They arrived in St. Maries two weeks after the projected Fourth of July show date. The plane, disassembled, was stored in a barn where repairs could be made. Among other damage, the fuselage had been ripped and torn. It would have to have new covering; an envelope of linen, suitably shaped and sewn, placed over the wood fuselage skelton and given many coats of nitrate dope.

While waiting for a new propeller and landing gear parts, Pang took his mother to the barn. On the way she asked;

"Clyde, what's all this talk about a covering for your fuselage?"

"It's a cloth covering, specially tailored . . . "

He was continuing his technical explanation when his mother picked up a piece of the torn material and rubbed her fingers over it.

"Why Clyde," she exclaimed, "this is just linen. Let's measure it right now. I can buy the material and sew it and you can have it on in a few hours."

She did, and it fit perfectly. Reed and Pang brushed on dope until the fabric pulled tight and smooth.

"Clyde, when do I get my ride for covering the fuselage?" his mother asked. She got the ride. Including stunts.

In a few weeks of flying from a local field, an improvement on the ball park where Pang had seen his first airplane, the two tyro barnstormers cleared $2,000 to add to the earnings from the communities they had covered earlier.

Pang went to Annis, the bank-director and pulled out a huge roll.

"Here's three thousand," he said. "First payment on the loan."

5

Fiasco at Coronado

THINGS HAD BEEN tough in San Diego. The dollars hadn't come as easily as they did in the first few weeks with the Jenny. So, to Pangborn and Reed, this looked like an easy $500. It was to be the first public attempt to transfer from a speeding automobile to an airplane. Ormer Locklear and Shirley Short, working for the movies in Los Angeles, had tried it and failed. They used a Case automobile, one of the fastest of the day, but still could not syncronize speed of the car and plane. Pangborn knew he could do it. He had already rehearsed it privately the day before.

The stunt was a promotion for the Del Coronado Hotel, that wooden structure of magnificient proportions located across a narrow arm of water from downtown San Diego. The manager, W.A. Tarquand, had put up the $500. More than 20,000 people had made their way to the Coronado Beach, coming across from San Diego on the tiny ferry, or by road around the bay. They had come, like the Romans to the Coliseum, in search of vicarious thrills.

And now Pangborn was standing on a platform at the rear of Al Lambla's high-wheeled Lozier tow car, hanging to a specially installed safety bar. Behind him somewhere his partner, Ralph Reed, was approaching rapidly in the Jenny, a wind-lashed ladder suspended below its wing. Lambla had the throttle to the floorboards. He was touching 60 miles an hour and his moustache was streamlined in the wind. It was the second run down the beach.

Pangborn considered the $500 as much as in his pocket. However, three elements were combining to forecast possible disaster, a denouement of which Pangborn was quite unaware.

First, Tarquand, the manager of the hotel, a Spreckles property, had told Pangborn: "When you practiced the stunt yesterday, it looked too easy when you climbed up the ladder from the car to the plane. You did it on the first try. With all that crowd out there, give them a little extra thrill. Make it look hard. Don't do the transfer until the third pass."

Second, Reed was flying from a part of the beach some distance from the demonstration site. He didn't know about a conference between Lambla and Pangborn. Lambla had said: "Look, Clyde, the idea of three passes is okay, except that the tide is coming in. There isn't any hard beach left to speak of. I'm going into soft sand and it's slowing me down. You've got to make the transfer on the second pass."

Third, J.O.Eychaner, a pilot out of Las Vegas, was flying his Aeromarine very close. He was not a part of the act and had moved in either in hope of such reflected glory as might be gleaned from his unscheduled participation, or to get a close-up view of the change from car to plane. He had crowded between Jim Hennessey, who was flying Morgan, the photographer from the San Diego Sun, and the Lozier.

The car sped madly on the thin strip of hard beach still available above the reaching fingers of the tide, Lambla fighting to avoid the soft sand. Eychaner moved in still closer, confusing Pangborn. Reed was flying too fast.

And then, the fourth element appeared. Reed, not knowing of the tide crisis, was flying so that the ladder Pangborn must seize was six feet to the left of the tow car. He thought this was a dry run; that the transfer would not be attempted until the third dash down the beach.

Pangborn leaned far to the left, his hands set to grasp the ladder, steel-muscled arms tense to hold.

He was a bit of infinity between everything that was wrong; Reed too fast, Eychaner where he should't be, Lambla too slow.

He grasped the ladder, tightening a vise-grip, felt the tug of a weight ten times as great as his own. He held to the taut ladder for an instant, his frantic wrists alive with instinctive self-preservation. Then it was too much.

He held nothing; was suspended in the air, traveling a-mile-a-minute.

Pang reaches far out for the ladder. The plane above is an interloper, not a part of the act, and its presence contributed to the accident.

Gravity and trajectory took over. He hit the sand ten feet below, a ball of flesh with legs and arms protruding.

The ball rolled, bounced, leaped, hit, lifted off the sand, lashed into it again, sailed once more through the air, finally slugged to a stop.

Meanwhile, Eychaner, the interloper, was in trouble with the Aeromarine. The engine had quit. Losing altitude and traveling fast he headed for the beach. When he touched down the plane swerved in the sand, hit an automobile, and careened into a bath house.

The show was over. The crowd had had the thrills it hoped for.

Reed later told Pangborn: "Pang, that was the damndest experience. For me, everything was in slow motion. I mean my speed, you reaching for the ladder, grabbing it and missing, the tow car plunging down the beach, your body going over and over, the crash of that Aeromarine into the car and the bath house."

But it hadn't been slow motion for Pangborn. Miraculously nothing in his body was broken. However, doctors found that he had severely injured his shoulder muscles, had stretched his left wrist in his efforts to cling to the ladder, had dislocated three vertebra, bruised the muscles of both hips and split the bone of one elbow. The results of the beating his body took were to remain with him for years.

His bounce to his feet and bow to the cheering crowd was sheer bravado. Al Lambla had spun the speeding car into a skid, throwing up sheets of sand, and dashed back to Pangborn. Pang's first words were: "I'm all right, Al, let's go back and do it again." Then he collapsed. He refused to go to a hospital; instead he slowly recovered at the Del Coronado Hotel as guest of the management.

Eychaner, evidently fearing that he was responsible for the accident, had retreated from his wrecked plane. He returned the next day to find that souvenier hunters—the bane of every crash—had stripped his craft like invading locusts.

With the $500 gone and the San Diego public displaying colossal indifference to the lonely Jenny and its two pilots on Dutch Flats, the fliers decided that they needed further stunts to attract attention and business.

Pangborn recalled an instance of his military training days when he had climbed out of the cockpit over Ellington Field to take a safety wire off the carburetor and thus permit a leaner mixture as he and his partner, Reed, flew the Hisso-Jenny on an altitude record attempt.

Now, at a remote area away from San Diego, with Reed flying, Pangborn got out of the cockpit. He worked his way along the fuselage until he was in front of an inboard leading strut, used the forward spar for a walk and went out to the left wing tip. Then he climbed to the top wing, stood, using the stub strut—a strengthener for the upper wing overhang—for a brace. He went back to the lower wing, maneuvered under it and gripped the wing skid with the "y" of his armpit, his feet running through the air. Very funny!

Pang casually strolling about the wings of his Jenny.

Pangborn was the second in the United States to do wing-walking. Ormer Locklear, the Hollywood stunt man, was the first. Third was Al Wilson, who later was killed, as was Locklear.

Certain that they had an attention gimmick, the two decided to try it on a Sunday over the Agua Caliente horse race track. They swept in low and Pangborn started his wing-walking. Spectators dived from the covered section of the grandstand to see better. The horses were parading to the post for the next race. Spooked by the crowd, the shouts, and the buzzing airplane, they took off in various directions, their unseated jockeys shaking fists at the careening Jenny.

It worked. Home-going race fans stopped at the field between the border and San Diego. Many clambered into the front cockpit of the Jenny for their first departure from solid ground. The take for the day was a welcome $200.

The Caliente foray convinced the partners that the main thing in a barnstormer's life was to attract attention. A ready opportunity was presented when the Prince of Wales (who later became Edward VIII and, after his abdication, the Duke of Windsor) came to San Diego. He was a member of the crew of H.M.S. Renown, making its first United States port of call.

The Prince and Governor William D. Stevens of California, as well as the usual dignitaries, were in a glass enclosure and San Diego's partly-filled stadium was listening quietly to the Prince's words.

From nowhere the Jenny swept down into the very bowels of the stadium. Pangborn climbed across the wings, stood on the top overhang, hung by his knees. The distraught Governor grasped the microphone of the loud-speakers: "If anybody knows how to signal that airplane to get out of here, do so."

The Prince of Wales: "No! No! I've never seen anything quite like this in my life. Let the airplane continue."

Two years later, on a more friendly occasion, Governor Stevens told Pangborn: "If I had had a gun that day, I would have shot you out of the sky."

Shortly after the San Diego stadium stunt Pang met his first "Tiny" Broadwick, and her sponsor, Charles Broadwick. This "Tiny" had made a tour during 1915 with Glenn L. Martin, an early barnstormer who later founded a highly successful airplane manufacturing company.

There were several "Tiny" Broadwicks, all protegees of "Professor" Broadwick. The first, more daring, most skilled and most unmindful of the hazards of the profession was a girl who later became Mrs. Georgia Brown. She was 19 years old in 1913 when she made her first jump. There in San Diego she came to Pangborn and explained:

"I need someone to fly me for a jump for the Chamber of Commerce at Ocean City."

She had her exhibition 'chute with her. Pang asked her if she had jumped it recently.

"Not exactly," she said. "The last time was at the fair here in San Diego in 1915."

"Five years!" Pang exclaimed. "Why, it may be mildewed. Anything might have happened. We'll have to make a sand bag drop with it as a test before I'll fly you."

A bag, filled to Tiny's estimated weight of 100 pounds, was dumped over the side. The 'chute popped cleanly and drifted down.

Pang flew Tiny over Ocean City at the designated hour. She had selected a vacant lot for her target. Slipping the shrouds, she made a perfect landing.

Annis, the bank director was visiting in San Diego and soon sensed that Pangborn and Reed were skimping on meals in their tight financial situation.

He called Pangborn in and said that, considering conditions, he and the other bank directors had decided to release Pangborn from any further payments.

"It's yours from here out, Clyde," he said.

If the stunt at Coronado was reckless, this one was weird; a strange concept growing out of intercollegiate rivalry. The intent was execution of the first bombing run in civilian airplane history. The target, Stanford University.

The two Jennys had taken off from Durant Field, Oakland, and had swept across the sluggish waters of San Francisco Bay. They were now cruising south along the peninsula, over San Francisco's bedroom communities of San Mateo, Burlingame and Redwood City.

Pangborn was at the controls of one of the Jennys; his passenger, a cheer leader from the University of California, was flying as observer on the mission. In the second plane were the pilot and the "bombardier." The latter, a graduate chemistry student, sat in the rear cockpit. In his lap were two glass globes, each 18 inches in diameter. The globes were filled with 10 per cent water and 90 per cent gasoline. Inside each globe was a cylinder, also of glass, containing metallic sodium which ignites on contact with water.

This was the day of college spirit, well before co-ed dormitories, athletic scholarships and sit-ins in the dean's office. Football players came voluntarily to the campus; many even graduated. The coach's word was law. Freshies wore green beanies. Students anguished when their teams lost; exulted in victory.

There were serpentine parades and pep rallies, and the greatest of the rallies was that staged annually on the Stanford Campus on the eve of the "Big Game" with California. Focus of the rally each year was a huge tepee-shaped pyre, the burning of which highlighted the game-eve gathering.

For weeks no loose piece of wood within miles of "The Farm"—as the Stanford campus was known—was safe as students scrounged material for the gigantic blaze. Day by day the huge pyramid of crates, boxes, beams, studs, railway ties and wooden bedsteads grew in height, until the students working on it appeared as pygmies.

For California students an annual objective was to set fire to the pile before the rally. Thus deprived of a pyrotechnic boost, Stanford would surely succumb to the Golden Bear. Infiltration, night forays, and other stratagems had been tried. Alas, the Stanford students, so far, had been too diligent in their determination to guard the pile.

Pangborn and the other pilot were primarily interested in the $100 they had been paid for the flight. The objective was to bomb and set fire to the giant woodpile.

Would the bomb, devised by the graduate student, explode as planned? A test run had been made the previous day. A duplicate bomb splashed down on a remote area of Durant Field. The metallic sodium ignited, exploding the gasoline. A fire ball as big as a house resulted. Yes, the bomb would work.

The two airplanes continued at low altitude until they reached the Stanford campus. Scrambling students were adding the last touches to the great accumulation of flammable material. It was to be lit that evening. Coach Walter Powell would exhort the students to support the team, the captain would make a brief talk, and rousing cheers would echo from the Palo Alto hills.

The Jenny with the bombs made a pass. The first globe, tossed by the student in the rear cockpit, overshot and landed well beyond the target. A conflagration like that of the day before resulted.

The students below, suddenly realizing that they were under a completely new type of attack, leaped and ran. They hit the ground and scattered as the Jenny made a second pass, dumping its lethal load.

Bulls-eye!

Weeks of effort and great plans for the evening went up in a technicolor of flame and smoke. In the best war-time tradition, the bomber plane swept low and zoomed over its disintegrating target. The observer in Pangborn's plane pounded the side of the fuselage in high glee. The coup had succeeded. California had drawn the first, major blood in the weekend rivalry.

The planes sped back to Oakland, even as an investigation got under way. It was to last for weeks. No one ever found out that the globes, the cylinders and the metallic sodium were missing from the chemistry labs of the University of California at Berkeley. Nor were the pilots and the airplanes identified, for airplanes in those days were not required to carry identification numbers.

The effort, however, was futile. Stanford won the big game, 38–0.

6

. . . and a Rolls Royce

WITHOUT HIS PARTNER Reed, who had departed for a regular job flying the air mail, Pangborn headed out with the Jenny to operate solo. At Long Beach he landed at Earl Daugherty's Chateau Thierry Field, a weed patch swept by the Pacific winds. Daugherty's mechanic was Ace Bragunier, who later flew in such great motion pictures as *Wings, Hell's Angels, Lilac Time,* and *Dawn Patrol.*

Winging north of Hollywood, Pang saw a green oasis against the grey hills. It was the one small town in the San Fernando Valley, which otherwise was an expanse of orchards and grain fields. The town was Burbank, named for Dr. David Burbank, dentist-rancher who owned most, if not all, the property within the city limits.

Had he had the gift of foresight, Pangborn would have seen that the land over which he flew was to become priceless. That Lockheed would establish its plant here and spew countless airplanes in World War II. That Universal Pictures Corporation, a speck at the southeast corner of the valley, would grow to world renown under Carl Laemle. That four brothers—the Warners—would start another internationally-famed studio. That hundreds of thousands would migrate over Cahuenga Pass from Hollywood and Los Angeles to gobble up subdivided farm lands. Not having that vision Pangborn looked instead to the railway tracks which he was following over the mountains into the San Joaquin Valley.

At Sacramento Pang talked himself into the passenger carrying concession at the state fair, in exchange for presenting a stunt flight daily. Jim Hennessey was signed on to fly the Jenny while Pang did his wing-walking exhibition.

During the fair Professor Charlie Broadwick said:

"I want you to jump Tiny. How about it?"

"Okay," Pang replied.

But this wasn't the original Tiny he had flown at San Diego. He was faced with a blonde, a luscious creature who started palpitations which required cultivation all during the fair. He took her up for her act each day, turning her loose at a point where she could drift down in front of the big grandstand to land on the race track—which she did with deft precision.

In mid-fair Pang rolled into an infield obstruction and broke the front spar of the left lower wing. He called a close friend stationed at nearby Mather Field.

"I need a lower left," Pang explained.

"That's easy," his friend replied. "Fly your crate out here and I'll put on a brand new one for free. But I can't truck a wing off the field without getting in a jam."

Pang found a panel in Sacramento, had to post a $600 bond to guarantee its return, and pay $150 rent.

Tiny Broderick clamboring aboard for a parachute jump from Pang's Jenny.

After the fair closed Pang flew out to Mather with the rented wing, got a new one, an undercarriage, struts, new tail surfaces, and other parts. He didn't feel too badly about this larceny for in a few months all supplies were to be burned, engines were battered with sledge hammers, and aircraft parts were sent to the dump heap. And, because of lack of congressional and public interest, complete airplanes were sold for $200 to $300 to any civilian who could raise the money.

After Sacramento, where $4,000 had been cleared, additional fairs up the valley were booked. At Redding, Hennessey observed the mountains looming toward the next stop, Yreka. "I'll be goddamned if I want to get goosed by a pine tree," he said as he quit his brief employment.

At Orland the fair committee scheduled Pang to taxi his plane down the main street—followed by the local girl scouts. The street was dirt. Pang envisioned the ire of the mothers when their dirty little darlings returned home.

In Yreka weariness caught up with plane and pilot. The tattered Jenny was parked near a graveyard. For some macabre reason most air fields seemed to be located near a cemetery. Pangborn went to bed with pneumonia.

As he recovered at the home of friends, he reviewed his life and pondered the future. So far flying had been his dominant interest, but any young man in twill breeches, Cordovan boots, and leather jacket was bound to attract feminine attention. Sure, there had been girls—of all kinds, shapes and sizes. One had put it most succinctly: "Aviators are different."

So far, the girls had come and gone in succession and as blurred as the memory of the fields from which he had flown. However, here in Yreka real romance challenged for the first time. This girl lived with her parents on a large stock ranch. She was indifferent to Pang's plane and his flying trappings. She was, however, warm and responsive to the young man himself. She was amused when he fashioned parachutes and dropped small gifts to her as he flew over the ranch.

A wife? A home and children? Responsibility for someone other than himself? Or a look at the other side of the mountain?

The girl's mother had said to him:

"Clyde, the man who marries my daughter will have a honeymoon in Euorpe, a Rolls Royce and a 10,000 acre ranch."

This to the lad whose mother had taken in sewing to support them during his early school days; the lad who had worked for $75 a month in the woods of Idaho, and who was eking a bare living as he barnstormed the western towns.

He was very fond of the girl. But there was that sky, the sky he had looked up to through the Idaho pines. There were plains, snow capped mountains—and horizons beyond.

Marriage would mean security, serenity, a fenced yard, routine. A retreat from the world that held surprise and fresh bloom as it leaped into life each morning.

The memory of lipstick on his lips, of a warm body at his side, Pang went to his helper, Shorty Orr.

"Let's get the hell out of here," he said.

"Why not?"

"There's a big air show coming up at Woodland. Fliers meet. First of its kind. We can have a lot of fun."

The Jenny had been made new; the engine overhauled, all wing and body surfaces recovered. Came the morning to leave. First the water was drained from the radiator, then the oil from the engine. A fire of oil-soaked waste warmed both. The sun reached over the Siskiyous; morning fog swirled around the base of Mount Shasta in frothy wisps. Fresh-mown first-cut alfalfa lent an aroma which blended with the more familiar smell of the heating oil.

Free from its too-long restraining tie-down, the Jenny took to the air. Pang raised his goggles to enjoy the full blast of the wind in his face; looked to the horizon beyond Shasta. How do you explain that this is more precious to a young man than a Rolls Royce, than rich acres, than love?

Eventually the girl got smart. She married another fellow, not a barnstormer. Presumably he collected the car and the ranch.

The Yolo County Air Meet of 1921—an innovation to be repeated through the years—had attracted a score of planes and pilots seemingly from nowhere. Among those who gathered were:

The genial Major H. H. (Hap) Arnold; Major Reed Chambers, World War I ace; Frank (Spook) Clarke; Gil Budwig; Matty Laird, whose company was to launch the Laird "Speedwing," and his pilot, George E. (Buck) Weaver, whose Weaver Aviation Company was to be shortened into the widely-known "Waco;" Pang's close friend Captain Lowell Smith, yet to gain national fame; Emory Rogers; Lt. Johnny Benton, who was to die in an Army formation flight over Buenos Aires.

Still others were Lt. H. H. Halverson, later an Air Corps general; the Jacuzzi brothers of propeller fame, in their sensational new high-wing monoplane; Monte Mouton, Mike Doolin, and Walter Varney, flying circus and airline pioneer.

Matty Laird and his new airplane stole the show, dominating the Fokker D7s, Curtiss Eagles, DHs, Standards, Jennys, an Ansaldo, Ballila, and the Jacuzzi. Pangborn managed a second in one of the races and collected $50.

Then down to San Francisco and competition for the few dollars available. A ride here and a ride there, slow dollars. Enough to eat on, if you didn't mind the grease joints and 50-cent dinners.

Pangborn had painted his name on the upper wing of his plane to exploit his identification as "Upside-Down Pang." When he was flying on his back the name was prominent to those on the ground.

Intrigued by the novelty of the upside-down caper, Lou Hutt, an enterprising and inventive newsreel photographer, forever on the alert for features he might sell to Pathe News or other of the news reels featured in the nation's theatres, came to Pangborn with an inspiration and offer of $100.

Hutt proposed to strap himself and his big camera in Pang's plane. Pang would fly upside-down. Another plane, piloted by Jay Fetters, would fly right-side-up with a camera pal. The two photographers would take movies of each other.

At 3,000 feet Pang dived, pulled into a half-loop and was upside-down. Fetters moved in and Lou and his pal cranked with abandon. With Hutt and his camera in the rear seat the plane was tail heavy; was wallowing all over the sky. Still Pang held on and on—far too long. The starved engine quit. He dead-sticked, still upside down, west of San Francisco's Twin Peaks. Finally he rolled out, stalled down to a weed-strewn sand dune and flipped into a gully, severely damaging one wing and smashing the propeller.

The $100 Hutt paid for the flight hardly covered the cost of repairs. Hutt was to figure in another spectacular stunt later.

Chasing wild ducks; strange job for an airplane. For $1.00 an acre Pangborn buzzed the rice fields of Colusa County. The farmers weren't concerned with what the ducks might eat, it was the rice they knocked down as they came in to land. Pang's job was to keep them from landing. Another pilot of the duck patrol was Charles Kingsford-Smith, later to be knighted for his aerial exploits which included the dramatic flight of The Southern Cross from the United States to Australia.

Another lucrative job simply fell into Pangborn's lap. His friend, Danny Davidson, came to him and said:

"Pang. I've just cracked up my plane. I've got three Chinese students sent over here by Sun Yat Sen. They are ensigns in the Chinese navy. He wants 'em to learn to fly. They are Wong Ping Tung, Nip Kai Hei, and a Honolulu Chinese, K. Y. Young. They're shaping up. You take over the contract and I won't charge you a damn cent."

The Chinese pay grossed $300 a week. Pangborn soloed each of the students, gave them a total of 20 hours each. They provided a good living for their instructor over a two months period. When they had finished, Wong said:

"You should come to China. There are many opportunities."

China seemed a great distance away across the vast expanse of the Pacific. With thanks, Pang said no to the suggestion.

Wong Ping Tung became the first commanding general of the Chinese Air Force, and later an air attache at the Chinese embassy in Washington, D.C. Nip Kai Hei became a top executive in Chinese National Airways and asked Pangborn to join him as manager of the concern's operations. Again the answer was no. Young became a bemedaled Colonel under Wong.

With the Chinese bonanza exhausted and dollars again hard to come by, Pangborn chanced to meet Van Gates at the Marina in San Francisco. After recalling their first meeting on the blackened grass in Ashland, Gates said:

"Pang, I want to talk to you. You can handle an airplane. How about dinner with Hazel and me?"

Over the meal Gates got down to business. "Look Pang, my

partner Lowell Yerex and I need a good stunt pilot. I've got a contract to stage a night fireworks exhibition for the 'Days of '49' celebration at Sacramento. I'll give you a percentage if you will fly it."

"Fine," Pang said.

The Jenny was loaded with fireworks; Roman candles filled with golden fire known as "waterfall," magnesium flares on the wingtips, various size bombs in Pang's lap. Over the capitol he lit the first bomb, dropped it overboard. That blast followed by smaller ones gave the effect of a sudden summer storm with its zig-zag lightning and rolling thunder. Lighting the fuses to the Roman candles, Pang looped repeatedly, the golden fire streaming hundreds of feet behind him. Finally the magnesium flares lit the entire city.

In the next six years Pangborn was to make more than 300 fireworks flights. At one time he had more night-time flying hours than many air-mail pilots who specialized in night operations.

And thus, rather casually, began an association of the promotional genius of Gates, the flying skill of Pangborn, and the tight-fisted financial management of Yerex, combining to build the greatest of the flying circuses.

7

Gates: Short-Fused Powder Keg

"THE P. T. BARNUM OF AVIATION," and "America's greatest aerial showman." These were but two of the superlatives accorded Ivan R. Gates in a two-page feature in the New York News. The article was written by Sloan (Cub) Taylor, pilot and aviation writer.

Gates was born at Rockford, Michigan on January 15, 1890. His grandfather, a Baptist clergyman, hoped he would enter the ministry. His father wanted him to prepare for the Naval Academy at Annapolis. Van disappointed both by dropping out of high school after three years and going to California. He became interested in auto racing and achieved some degree of success on the dirt-track circuit. Later he claimed to have bought a cracked-up airplane and to have launched himself on an air career. If he did in fact buy the plane, someone else flew it, for Gates did not know how to fly at that time.

The only known picture of Ivan Gates near an early-day plane shows him at the controls of an ancient Curtiss pusher. He sits in the pilot's seat, his left hand on the wheel. He has a broad smile. His cap is on backward. His suit is a violent pin-stripe. He had labeled the picture "Richmond, 1913—Curtiss Pusher." He had forgotten goggles. The plane quite obviously is very solidly on the ground.

His forte, however, lay not in performance, but in promotion at which he was a genius. Weaver of tall tales that would put Baron

Ivan R. Gates sitting at the controls of a Curtiss pusher.

Munchausen to shame, somehow Gates first convinced himself that his dreams were real.

He would wrap a lackluster pilot and a tired, faded airplane in gossamer and present the combination to press and public so that the stench of burned oil and gas was perfume and the sky the most exciting, dangerous, wonderful, fantastic and beautiful place in the universe.

This was the enigmatic man who could induce newspapers to produce reams of copy about him and his aerial comrades; who could keep commercial aviation alive for more than a decade when national indifference would have buried it; who could bring out a hundred thousand people to see three asthmatic, staggering planes in action; who could stage shows for the Army Air Service they couldn't put on for themselves; who could cut a million dollar path across the sky of the nation.

Drunk or sober, he advanced a mythical throttle, lifted himself on mental wings, heard and felt the beat of the propeller, landed from his chimerical sky and sprayed the dew from the grass as his phantom wheels touched down.

Gates was neither tall nor short; possibly five feet, ten inches. He was not fat nor thin. He had a pug nose. When he smiled, his eyes closed to slits. They did the same when he was angry. A charmer and a sadist; at once parsimonious and overgenerous; Gates was mercurial; totally unpredictable.

Under Gates' fantasizing his early partner, Lowell Yerex, bloomed as an ace of World War I who had shot down seven enemy planes and who had the ability to "run the gamut of war acrobatics."

Later Yerex told Pangborn of his short military career. He had enlisted in the British Royal Flying Corps and after brief training was sent to the front. Very soon, without bringing down a single German plane, he was shot down and captured. He spent the remainder of the war in a prison camp. On discharge from the service he came to the United States, met Gates and formed a partnership of sorts in which he had the controlling interest. Although Gates gave the impression that he was the boss, it was the stuttering Yerex who managed the purse with tight fist.

Pangborn, too, was accorded a mythical career. According to Gates, Pang was the "Peck's Bad Boy" of the Air Service. Although a brilliant instructor, he had a weakness for knocking balls off flag poles, a disregard for flying rules, and indulged in other escapades which prevented his being sent overseas.

Thornton ("Jinx") Jenkins, the little wing-walker who had a wife and son in Los Angeles, soon found that he was Hollywood's greatest stunt man—he had not only performed in all films requiring hazardous work, but had actually saved the lives of at least two stars.

Under Gates a half-hundred pilots, wing-walkers, parachute-jumpers, mechanics and advance men were to roam the highways of the sky. They were to caper in the sunshine, freeze in high mountain cold, go hungry in the lean winter months and squander the money which on rare occasions poured into their thin pockets. They were to light fires in the rising sun to warm themselves and the oil and water for their engines; they were to feel the icy fingers of wind against their faces in the open cockpits as they hopped from town to town. They would sear in summer heat and find brief joy in the fragrant fields of spring.

As he made the hop-scotch moves from city to city, Gates was accompanied by his faithful wife Hazel. Short, brunette, her every look bespoke her love for Van, though she often felt the wrath of his drunken rages and was well aware of his pursuit of other women. Rarely, on those occasions when even her amazing tolerance level was exceeded, Hazel would take off. First, however, she always told Pangborn where she was going, as she had done on this occasion.

Gates summoned Pangborn to his room.

"Pang, Hazel's left me. Where is she?"

"I don't know, Van."

"You've got to know. Look. I'm going crazy. I know I am. I can prove it."

Van had always been generous in buying Hazel clothes. She even had a beautiful mink coat.

Van pulled out the drawers of a chest. Every article of clothing, all obviously feminine, had been torn into small pieces. The mink coat was a bedraggled sight.

"I've ripped up all her clothes, Pang, every goddamn thing she left. Now you know I'm crazy. If you don't tell me where she is, I'll jump out the window!"

Pangborn phoned Hazel, explaining Van's condition and persuaded her to talk to him. Later, in the lobby Gates appeared very happy, very grateful, and, not surprisingly, thoroughly sloshed. Hazel, he said, had forgiven him and was returning.

"I'm a great little salesman," he said, as his eyes pinched to their characteristic slit. "By God, I talked to her for an hour."

The hotel had a long flight of stairs, straight from the second floor to the ground level. The next day Pang encountered Hazel in the lobby. Her nose was smashed and swollen; she had a black eye. He asked her what had happened.

"I tripped and fell down the stairs," she said, pointing.

Pang knew that a fall down that flight would have resulted in more serious injury; that these were man inflicted. No doubt Van had been expressing his gratitude for Hazel's return. Pang pondered the mysteries, the vagaries of woman's love.

On a few occasions Gates went beyond his depth. A diner in Seneca Falls, New York, refused him permission to display a circus halfsheet advertisement in its window.

"Get that damned thing outta here," the owner told the bill poster. "Your pilots are a bunch of yellow-bellies; they won't fly at night."

Gates blew a gasket when he learned of the incident. Quite drunk, he invaded the diner.

"Nobody can call my pilots yellow," he announced. "I'll whip any son-of-a-bitch in this joint."

A long, lean gent folded his napkin very carefully, rose gracefully from his stool and said in a low, unhurried voice:

"I guess that means me."

Gates charged. Wham! Down he went.

He got up. Wham! He went down a second time.

He got up a third time. Wham!

This time he stayed down.

The next day his eyes were permanent slits. His lips were puffy and heavy. Someone asked him what had happened.

"My old failing," he mumbled. "I chose the wrong guy—picked an old pro."

And then there was "Buck" McKinney, who after he'd been told repeatedly not to fly cross-country after dark, ran out of gas one black night and cracked up on the banks of the Hackensack River. When Gates heard of the crash his mental crankshaft shattered. On arrival at the scene he literally ran amok. In his fury he pulled out a packet of matches and set the plane on fire.

"Goddamn it! Goddamn it!" he kept repeating as he watched the devouring flames.

Once Gates wanted to get in touch with his advance man in Gainesville, Florida. Not knowing where the man was staying he used the standard form for such occasions and addressed his Western Union wire "Try hotels." This, of course, meant to call each hotel until the man was located and the message delivered.

Shortly a call came and a very sweet, feminine voice said:

"I'm sorry, Mr. Gates, but there is no 'Try' hotel in Gainesville."

Gates tore the telephone from the wall, jumped on it, and never again used Western Union.

Yet this was the man who could mesmerize tough newspaper editors, who could go out and line up an exhibition, a booking, a sponsor, a field to fly from, promote free gasoline or dream up a stunt that would give a vicarious thrill to a quarter million people. Maybe you had to be crazy to create the greatest flying circus in the world.

8

Wes May Joins Up

WHEN PRESENT WING-WALKER IS KILLED, I WANT THE JOB. Pangborn took the cheerful message from his pocket and noted the name signed to it: WESLEY MAY. The dire event predicted in the message had occurred only hours earlier.

The circus was performing under auspices of the San Jose, California, Aero Squadron. Supervising was Major William J. Cross, commanding officer of the squadron, while Gates was the show's "Director-General," a title he loved.

Pilots of the circus included Yerex, in a Hispano-Squiza Standard; Billy Morris in a rebuilt Lincoln Standard; Captain Sam Purcell in a Curtiss R; Morris in an Italian Ansaldo; Emmett Tanner in a Curtiss Special; Dick Doane in a Curtiss JN4D; Oscar Natley in a Canadian "Canuck" and Pangborn in his Jenny.

Climax of the show for the 20,000 people who had paid 50 cents each for a viewing spot was to be the 3,000 foot parachute jump by Jinx Jenkins, the young wing-walker from Los Angeles. He was being flown by Yerex.

Pangborn was standing with Hazel Gates and a charming girl whom he considered his current opportunity. The plane circled and, at 3,000 feet, Yerex leveled off. Pang waited for the white canopy to put a dot above the X which would be Jenkins.

The crowd, tense in the afternoon sunshine, "aahed" as Jenkins' body was dark against a slow-floating cloud. He began the cometing arc which would close the show. Behind him trailed a broken, wind-whipped streamer which should have been a parachute. Down he came against the unsustaining air.

Pang whirled to Hazel and the girl.

"Turn your backs," he snapped.

He watched the gyrating body of Jenkins, fighting against the last split second. He hit a thousand feet away, a tangled ball of broken bones and torn flesh.

This was not the first time Pangborn had seen death reach its fingers into the sky. He feared death and thus gave it full respect. In his wing-walking stunts he always roped or wired the wing-tip skids for safety before placing his weight on them.

The wing skid on a Jenny was a curved piece of light tubing on the under side of the outboard end of each lower wing. The ends of the tubing fit into metal sockets with bolts through to hold them in place. The purpose of the skid was to absorb the shock should a wing touch the ground.

Pang was flying into Sid Chaplin Field, facing Wilshire Boulevard in Los Angeles. As he descended he noted that a wing-walking show was going on. The pilot leveled while the wing-walker made his way across the lower panel, lowered himself to the skid and hung by one hand. Pang banked away to clear the area because no pilot barged into an air show.

As he watched, the wing-walker started to pull himself up when suddenly the entire skid assembly gave way. He seemed to hurl the skid from him as he fell, speeding faster and faster in a long arc. He hit hard.

Re-reading the macabre message, following Jenkins' death Pang wired May to join the circus as its new wing-walker. They had first met when May worked as mechanic and roustabout for Ormer Locklear. May, born in Oregon, had been a vaudeville tumbler and motorcycle racer. He was absolutely without fear and as a consequence, careless.

He was a persistent user of snuff. Like a good Scandinavian, he would take a generous portion between thumb and forefinger, slip it inside his lower lip and announce: "Here's where we separate the men from the boys."

May's snuff and his comment were known wherever pilots gathered. Pang was flying him over Mather Field during an air show. May was sitting on the top wing, completely relaxed. Yerex was lining up his plane for the plane-change. May grinned down at Pang, fished out his snuff box, pointed to it as Pang read his lips: "Here's where we separate the men from the boys."

Yerex came in just above Pang's plane. May rose, grabbed the suspended ladder and scrambled up into the upper ship.

May was about five feet, eleven. He had the muscles of a weight-lifter. His agile mind was constantly devising new aerial stunts. That imagery produced the first mid-air refueling. With a five-gallon can of gasoline strapped to his back, he had climbed up a ladder from one airplane to another, and poured the fuel into the second plane's tank.

Flying with Pangborn, May would ease himself out onto the engine after Pang had stopped it by shutting off the ignition. May would then crank the propeller for a re-start while straddling the engine like a "buster" aboard a bronco. At first the sparkplugs were taped to avoid giving May a husky shock in the posterior. He protested:

John W. Underwood photo collection.

Wesley May, with a five-gallon can of gas strapped to his back, transferring to another plane.

"Hey, that's no fun. Let me have the heat on my tail."

May conceived the "breakaway" which became a standard stunt with the circus. He would seemingly plunge from the lower wing toward his death. After a drop of about ten feet a rope around his ankle would stop the fall. Then with amazing coordination and his extraordinary strength he would pull himself back up the rope to the airplane. Scores of women would faint as they saw May slip from the wing.

One day Lou Hutt, the imaginative motion picture cameraman, came to Pangborn and asked: "Could you get a man who would ride a bicycle across the top wing of an airplane while I shot from another plane?"

Pang answered: "Wes May is your man."

May agreed with alacrity.

First a plywood catwalk was laid over the leading spar of Yerex's top wing. Yerex suggested running a wire along this walk with a ring sliding on it. A safety wire would go from the ring to the bicycle.

"You're not going to make a sissy out of me," May exploded.

"Look dope," Yerex told him, "I'm not trying to bust up your silly damned ethics. I just don't like the idea of being smacked by a bicycle while I'm flying a half mile up. The safety wire goes to the bike, not to you."

May agreed, mumbling to himself about pilots without "guts."

The bike was gotten up onto the wing. May climbed into the front cockpit, took a pinch of snuff and said: "Okay, let's go."

Yerex took off. Hutt and his camera were in another ship. His plan was to stand on the engine, facing backwards. He had mounted his camera's tripod firmly on the center section of the wing. Yerex and May were to come in directly behind the camera plane and then May, on signal, was to pedal the bike from wing-tip to wing-tip.

Hutt wanted Yerex to move closer and started to signal by waving his arms. One wind-whipped hand got into the propeller arc and the prop sliced off a finger.

Bleeding heavily and pale with pain, Hutt clung to the tradition that "the shot comes first." He got it, a handkerchief staunching the flow of blood from the severed digit.

"I'd like to find that finger," Hutt grumbled after the plane landed. While a temporary bandage was applied, search was made for the finger and a mechanic found it caught under a guy wire.

"We'd better give it a proper burial," someone suggested. A small box was found, a hole dug and with profane solemnities the "casket" was lowered and covered with dirt. Only then would Hutt agree to go to a hospital. The films of May's bicycle ride were a sensation when shown in theatres across the country.

Gates had done it again. This time it was an Air Show at Crissy Field in San Francisco. Sponsorship was by the Army Air Services, which had provided the field, the crowd security, ticket takers, and a supporting troupe of 100 military aircraft from Mather Field at Sacramento. The officer in charge was Major H. H. (Hap) Arnold, Lieutenant Halverson his assistant air officer. Major George H. Brett was the Crissy Field Post Commander. Gates, as usual, was the "Director-General" of the show which had attracted more than 100,000 people.

Army brass had turned out in force and included pilots who later became generals, wrote records in the flying book, and were honored

Major H. H. "Hap" Arnold, left, with Major George Brett and Major Frank Lahm at the Crissy Field Air Show, 1921. Arnold later became Commanding General of the U.S. Air Force.

after death by having military fields named for them. Among those in attendance were:

Captain Lowell H. Smith, who two years later led the famous Army "Round-the-World" flight; Lt. Russell L. Maughan, soon to win fame with his dawn-to-dusk flight across the nation; Major B. W. Atkinson, for whom Atkinson Field is named; Captain F. I. Eglin, similarly honored in Eglin Field; Lt. A. E. Waller, his achievements marked by Waller Field, Trinidad. Others were Lt. John A. Benton, Lt. Ned Schram, Lt. F. F. Gullet, Lt. George A. McHenry, and Lt. W. V. Maxwell.

Following various formation flights and precision maneuvers by the military, Lt. Maxwell, officer of the day, told Pangborn:

"Do your stuff, Pang."

Pang put everything he had into it. He flew upside-down, did loops, slow rolls, whip stalls, and wound up with a chandelle and a high speed dive to within five feet of the ground. As he landed and killed his engine he heard Major Brett shout:

"Send that man over to me!"

"Young man, you have violated every regulation of this field. You are grounded!"

"But, Sir!" Pang protested, "everybody knows my show, knows what I do. Lt. Maxwell, your officer of the day, told me to 'do my stuff.' I simply did it."

"I can't help that. Every reserve squadron in the country will be advised that you are grounded."

This meant that Pang could no longer fly from Crissy Field, and that, as a reserve officer, he could no longer borrow government planes. He walked away with drooping shoulders while the show went on.

The climax again was to be the 3,000-foot parachute jump, this time by May. As he climbed into the plane he told Yerex:

"Don't drop me in the bay. I don't want to get wet."

He followed the light-hearted remark with the usual pinch of snuff. Yerex taxied out. Wes waved, and the Standard's nose sought the sky. One thousand—two—three.

Wes jumped—fell. The 'chute popped. He drifted with the wind whipping in through the Golden Gate. He was missing the water. But he was also missing the field, which was close to the usual cemetery.

This time it was the military burial ground of the Presidio. The wind drifted Wes beyond the field, despite his efforts to slip to a landing. He slammed into an eucalyptus tree—grabbed a limb forty feet off the ground.

Pang watching, gasped: "Thank God."

But as the sustaining 'chute collapsed and transferred Wes's weight to the tree, the limb snapped. He plunged downward. Pang and the others who rushed to the cemetery found Wes buckled over a headstone. An Army ambulance sped him to a hospital in the city.

After the spectators had streamed homeward and the planes had been tied down at the Marina, Yerex and Pang sought out Gates.

"We'd better get the hell down to the hospital and find out how Wes is."

They found him in bed, his snuff box on the table beside him. Wes wise-cracked as usual. He asked Yerex to hand him the box, put a generous portion inside his lower lip, grimaced with the pain of the effort.

"So we separate the men from the boys again," he said. "I'll be out of here in a couple of days."

Wes May died at 9 p.m. that evening.

9

The Great Diavalo

THE MORNING AFTER Wesley May's death Gates called a conference in his hotel room.

"Look, I'm sorry for Wes, but this death business is costing me money. First Jenkins, and now May. I have bills printed by the thousands. I had to throw away great bunches when Jinx died. I had more printed when we took on Wes. Now I've lost my shirt on this last batch. What the hell are we going to do?"

It was characteristic that Gates referred to "his" money, but when there was a problem it was "ours."

After some thought, Pangborn said:

"We need a common name, you could call it a trade name. A name we can give to any wing-walker or parachute jumper."

"That's it, Pang," Gates responded with enthusiasm. "I remember when I was a kid seeing 'Diavalo.' He worked in a circus and looped a bicycle by going down an inclined runway that ended in a circle. The name is 'Eyetalian,' or something."

"Sounds good," Yerex agreed. "If Diavalo gets killed, we just get another one."

"Agreed then," Gates said. "Now we need another wing-walker. Lad named Freddie Lund, down at Sid Chaplin Field, has written asking for a job."

Thus it was that Freddie Lund, former cowboy and rodeo rider, joined the circus to become the first of many Diavalos. Freddie was light, fleet and sure in every action. He loved aviation. He had an eagle beak and he developed the flying abilities of that powerful, graceful bird.

Financial arrangements for the highly successful Crissy Field show had followed the established pattern. All expenses were charged against receipts and then the money was split on the established formula. The sponsoring body, in this case the Army Relief Fund, got 40 per cent, while Gates got 60 per cent. The 40 per cent which went to the sponsors in turn found its way into relief, welfare, hospital and mess funds.

Gates, of course, took his own cut first as advance man, setting up the shows, and then as "Director-General." The pilots and wing-walkers got their share, each assigned a percentage depending on his contribution to the performance. On a show drawing 20,000 cash customers paying $10,000 Pangborn could expect up to $750. A man

A "Diavalo" prepares to make a ladder exchange to the upper plane.

doing both wing-walking and parachute-jumping would get $200 in addition to his regular wages as mechanic.

With his characteristic indifference to money, Pangborn would leave much of his take to accumulate with Yerex, keeper of the purse. What he drew above current living expenses he would bank wherever he might be, and so acquired accounts in a number of widely scattered communities. Following the Crissy Field show he said to Yerex:

"Lowell, you owe me about two thousand dollars. How about it?"

Yerex stuttered in confusion:

"Pang, I-I-I haven't got it. You know, expenses have been high and I-I-I'm building up another Standard. It is costing me m-m-money."

"You don't understand," Pang persisted. "You owe me two grand."

"I'll g-g-give you the Standard I've been f-f-flying. It's better than your Jenny."

"Okay, give me a bill of sale."

The Jenny had been tied down at the Marina. Pang moved it into a small building, took off the wings, and tilted it up on its nose to save space. He and the Jenny had performed over the heads of more than a million people, had carried thousands on their first flights, had played tag with clouds, and had dipped into quiet mountain valleys, had dared the spume flicked from the sea's waves. They had won fame, if not fortune. And now the Jenny was being given a rest. In the quiet of the shed Pang took a final look at his friend—his first love—who had given him freedom from the workaday world for more than three years. "This isn't the end," he said. "I'll be back in six months."

With the new Standard, Pangborn became one of the seven pilots who inaugurated the first scheduled airline between San Francisco and Los Angeles. Today service between the two cities is on an around-the-clock commuter basis; thousands fly between the two cities each day. In 1922 the proposed service was headline news of spectacular import.

There were seven airplanes—Lincoln Standards—each of which could carry four passengers. Four of the planes had "long range" tanks and three, Pang was told, had "short range" tanks. The explanation confused him.

The other pilots, in addition to Pangborn, were "Loop-the-loop" Murphy, Clevenger, Davis, Tanner, Fowler and Dawson. The airline was the most ambitious conceived up to that time.

First premonition of what was to come should have been noted when Clevenger took one of the planes for a test flight. He took off from the Marina, circled out over the bay in a wide, sloppy, skidding turn.

"Something's wrong," a mechanic shouted. Clevenger was usually as smooth as silk at the controls; obviously he was having difficulty. Somehow he brought the plane in and got it on the ground.

"No ailerons," he said.

An examination showed that his control horn was broken.

On opening day for the service the seven planes were on the line at the Marina. The promotion had been effective; each of the planes was filled with passengers. Pang's four included a newsreel cameraman. He was to record the flight, from take-off to landing, to demonstrate that air travel had arrived. Had there been a photographer in each of the planes they would have recorded a fiasco of catastrophic dimensions.

Murphy was the first casualty. He landed with a dead engine on Crissy Field, a full two miles from the starting point. Pangborn's engine expired over Gilroy when a connecting rod broke. The passengers, including the cameraman and his equipment, were sprayed with oil. Davis went down at San Jose. Tanner landed at Salinas and went over on his back, his shaken passengers escaping without injury. Dawson lost his propeller, and glided, dead-stick, into a farmer's field near Santa Barbara. Fowler was in sight of Sid Chaplin Field when he was forced down.

Clevenger was the only one to make it all the way to Los Angeles. Not only that; he gassed and flew back to the Marina in San Francisco. The one-day life of the airlines was undoubtedly the shortest of any airline in aviation history.

It was some time later before the innocent Pangborn learned that the airline's real purpose was to “import” liquor from Tijuana. The “short range” tanks on the three airplanes were to permit them to carry extra cargo in the form of another quickly detachable tank containing whiskey. In emergency the pilot could fly out over the ocean and jettison the tank of illegal liquor.

Swede Meyerhoffer rented one of the planes to carry passengers, assuming it had the normal “long range” tanks. He ran out of fuel over the mountains, side-slipped and stalled down into heavy timber, wrecking the plane but without injury to his passengers or himself.

Some time later Swede rented a plane from young Walter Varney, who was to pioneer the first successful airline up and down the Pacific Coast. Swede took off for the boondocks. At one of the remote spots the Varney mechanic who accompanied him tried to crank his engine.

“Get outta there,” Swede exclaimed. “I crank my own damn windmill!”

He did. But he was slightly off balance. The first turn of the propeller hit his shoulder. He fell forward into the propeller arc. A blade caught his back, causing serious internal injuries from which he died.

Varney had instructed the mechanic to make his telegrams brief, ten words or less. Following the accident the mechanic wired:

“Swede cranked prop. Prop killed Swede. Send new prop.”

Varney was so fascinated by the nine-word telegram that he had it enlarged and hung it in his office even as his airline expanded into its later affluence.

The Standard and its Hispano-Suiza engine hadn't yet learned that Pangborn was the master. So the three were pitching, rolling and wallowing in the hot air above the Nevada desert between Reno and Winnemucca. In the wind strumming the brace wires, in the beat of the engine, Pang heard a tune: ‘I'm Forever Chasing Rainbows.” He had heard it the night before with Frank Mansfield and the two girls in San Francisco.

He pondered: "Why does a man in his right mind stay up all night, drive up to Twin Peaks and watch the sun rise? Because he is still in his twenties, because each day is new and fresh, because there is a girl beside him, because he isn't able to let himself be surrounded by a cottage, a picket fence and howling little monsters?"

That was the trouble with the romance in Yreka; that threat of claustrophobia which comes with a cottage. There's the song again. "Some fellows find the sunshine; I always seem to find the rain."

Below were the rails stretching to Promontory, Utah, where they joined the steel from the east which, in 1867, had fulfilled the dream of Abraham Lincoln for a transcontinental railroad. Still visible, but faint, were the ruts made by the wagons of the pioneers who trekked across this barren waste at a mere ten or fifteen miles a day. There, far to the north, was the Oregon Trail which reminded Pang of Idaho, the graceful pines, St. Maries and his mother. He had been sending her money regularly; he would like to see her.

Right now he had a date in Salt Lake City where Gates had booked a night fireworks exhibition over the lagoon, north of the city and west of Bountiful. It had seemed prudent for the circus to leave California and head for the mountain country for several reasons.

First, there was the depression. Second, people on the coast were sated with flying; barnstormers were literally starving. Finally there were the stunts. Pangborn felt equally at fault with the others for the latter.

It had started when Pangborn slammed into the beach at Coronado. There was an editorial which said:

"Legislation against unnecessary exhibitions like that on Coronado last Sunday, in which a finely trained and competent aviator nearly lost his life to please a popular fancy, would not be foolish legislation."

Then, after the death of Wesley May, a San Francisco paper editorialized:

"Immediate arrest of aviators attempting 'stunt flying' or 'wing-walking' has been ordered by the State Aviation Board. Stunts result in the death of fliers. Daredevil flying performs no useful purpose and, on the contrary, creates a popular distrust of airplanes and aviation in general."

Pangborn remembered the bombs dumped on the great pile of

wood to wreck Stanford's pep rally. He recalled when one of his friends took two passengers down into the University of California stadium at Berkeley to break up a football game by bouncing his wheels in the middle of the gridiron. He sees Ormer Locklear walking wings just above the trolley wires on Market Street in San Francisco.

Perhaps here in the mountains the people, and the press, will be more tolerant. As he came in over the Great Salt Lake and circled the city, Pang saw the Mormon temple and tabernacle; the statue of Brigham Young looking out over the beautiful city and fertile fields where there had been only sage brush when the Mormons arrived.

Shortly after Pang landed, Gates appeared. He had a stranger in tow. Both were drunk. Very drunk.

"Want you meet Casey," Gates mumbled. "J. C. Casey. New advance man. Have to have advance man. Now I'm director-general."

"I need five dollars," the swaying, unsteady Gates continued. "Under agreement, me and Yerex, Pangborn pays me five dollars a day."

To get rid of him, Pang fished out the five dollars, then joined Freddie in attaching the fireworks for the night display. Looking up he saw Gates and Casey wrestling with one of the gasoline drums. Pang had paid for it with his own money. Finally, in their drunken clumsiness they upset the barrel. Fuel poured on to the ground. Hammer in hand, Pang went for Gates.

"Look, you drunken son-of-a-bitch, that's my gasoline. Lay off!"

"Jeesus!" Gates bellowed as he backed away. "Casey an' me . . . we gotta go t'the newspapers. Need th' gas . . ."

Gates continued to retreat and was gone by the time LaMar Nelson came over to see what was going on. Nelson, a World War flier, was a secretary to Governor Charles R. Maybe of Utah. He had another man with him.

"I want you to meet Captain George," he said. "He might be helpful."

Captain George was to become General George, head of the Air Transport Command in World War II.

The Salt Lake City show went well, except for one difficulty. The lagoon was close to the lake. Guided by the moon, with mountains to the east and lake to the west, Pang became confused, as he looped and flew on his back. The moon was in the sky. But it was also mirrored in the waters of the great Salt Lake. Which was the real moon? Which way was up, which was down? Fortunately he chose right and landed safely.

There followed a succession of towns. One or two day stands, grab a bite to eat, a few hours sleep, then on to the next dusty field. Only rarely was there a break in the dull routine, such as that at St. George, Utah, capital of the "Dixie" which Brigham Young had ordered settled as he expanded the Mormon empire.

It was here that Pangborn encountered the most fascinating passenger of the thousands he flew in the decade of the circus. The man was stout, about 30, a chiropractor—and blind. He was from a family in which five of seven children had been born without sight. At the field on a mesa to the west above the town, he wandered aimlessly, curious about the strange contraption which had come to St. George.

"I want to see it," he said to Pangborn. "Show me."

Pang led him around the airplane, guided him as he felt the propeller, the wings, the tail surface.

"You know," he said, "I can tell the color of horses, although I have been blind since birth. I can tell the color and names of automobiles. . . ."

"There's a car behind you, about fifty feet," Pangborn said. "What is it?"

"A blue Buick. Somehow I know these things. It's mental telepathy, I think. I see what you see. I'd like to ride in your airplane—have a stunt ride."

"You don't know anything about my airplane."

He described it perfectly from propeller to rudder.

"Okay," Pang told him. "I'll give you a ride. Free."

It was the works; rolls, Immelmans, spins, loops, falling leaves, whipstalls.

The man's face was radiant as, on landing, he described every maneuver they had flown.

Except for the rare occasions, as at St. George, barnstorming was dull routine. All hands worked like drones, repairing the engines, stunting over the communities to attract attention, carrying passengers whenever they showed up, holding the parachute jump until dusk in order to keep potential passengers at the field, cleaning up, eating, and then falling exhausted into bed.

Working north and homeward, Pang led the show into Idaho. At Minidoka two major misfortunes befell him. On landing at night at this center of the famed Idaho potato country, Pangborn shattered a spar against an unseen post in the center of the field.

"That ain't nothing, nothing at all," a farmer said as he drove up to the wreck. "Heard ya buzzin'. You missed the town water tank by less than twenty feet. This ain't nothing."

The usual patch and repairs and the plane was ready for business. Still no one came. Inquiry established that the farmers had no money.

"Tell you what I'll do," one farmer said. "Potatoes are worth thirty-five cents a bushel. I'll bring out 15 bushels and put 'em on the field. You can sell 'em."

The idea caught on. Pang flew a long day, staging shows in between passenger flights. As evening descended he had a row of Idaho's finest potatoes nearly fifty feet long and four feet high.

"What in hell are you going to do with them?" Milt Girton, the parachute-jumper, asked.

"Sell 'em. Didn't you hear the farmer say they were worth thirty-five cents a bushel?"

"Look, chump, if the farmers couldn't sell 'em, how can you?"

Pang checked with local businessmen the next morning. Nobody wanted his potatoes. He and Milt headed west, leaving behind the pile of unwanted potatoes.

Rupert, Twin Falls, Gooding, Mountain Home, Boise. Then north to dip into the Clearwater valley and a brief stop at Orofino where Pang and his brother had smoked the "threefers." Familiar territory now, the sweep of the Bitter Root mountains, the narrow valleys with their clear, hastening streams. Over a final hump and down the St. Joe river to St. Maries where his mother was waiting at the field.

"Clyde, you've been gone quite a while."

She then declared that she hadn't flown for some time and asked for a stunt ride. She delighted in every mad twist of the cavorting plane. A flight certificate issued by Clyde to his mother attested that she had flown to an altitude of 5,000 feet and had done Immelmanns, three-turn spins and wing-overs.

Pang visited old friends at Kellogg and Wallace, flew over the smelter smokestack which he had climbed to measure with a chain, spotted the pond into which he had plunged after his wild ride down the flume. It was great to be home, but one must be free, free to look at the other side of the mountains which rolled eastward and south for hundreds of miles.

He and Milt headed south. In northern Arizona they paused briefly at Williams, Flagstaff, Winslow and Holbrook. At the later Pang saw a cold, dilapidated airplane. Lettered on its side was: "Clever Clevenger—Atlantic Ocean or Bust." Clevenger explained that he was accepting the "bust" and was going back to his favorite location, the Marina at San Francisco.

"By the way," he said to Pang, "did you know you've lost your Jenny?"

"What!"

"That's right. The building where you stored it burned down. Not a thing saved."

Pangborn felt that he had heard of the death of a friend.

In Phoenix Pangborn found a lone operator flying from the fair grounds. On the field he noted several Thomas-Morse Scouts which were tricky pursuit trainers powered with rotary engines. They had no regular carburetor, instead a mixture control which was difficult to adjust. The "throttle" control was a blip button on top of the stick which cut out the magnetos, thus retarding the engine.

One of the Thomas-Morses—a modified two-seater—proved to be the property of Lynn Lockhart, a friend of Pang's.

"I'm just about to paint my Scout," he said. "I'll be flying it soon."

"Why not fly it first," Pang said, "and maybe you won't have to paint it."

Lockhart's eyes grew large.

"You mean it's not safe? Why this local pilot got us fellows to buy them in San Diego for a dime a dozen. He said he'd give us two hours of instruction and away we'd go."

"You'd 'go' all right," Pang said. "The Scouts are sensitive, they react fast to the controls and the engines are hard to handle. They were designed for pursuit pilots in the final stages of training. They aren't for amateur pilots."

Pangborn volunteered to fly Lockhart and show him what he was talking about. He took off, flew several stunts. He showed how the Scout would snap roll to one side, but was very difficult to roll to the other, because of the gyro effect of the rotary engine.

"You better get a lot more flying time before you try to fly this beast," Pang advised.

"Fly it! Hell, I'm going to burn it." Lockhart shouted.

10

Partners

THE LITTLE OLD LADY, obviously someone's grandmother, walked hesitantly toward the DeHavilland biplane on the field at Fort Bliss, a few miles from El Paso. The idling engine was turning the propeller over slowly.

The circus, a feature of the week-long El Paso Jubilee, was operating under auspices of the Border Patrol. The Patrol was a collection of Army fliers assigned to chase smugglers, aliens, bootleggers, cattle rustlers, and anything else that looked suspicious, in which category the fliers gratuitously included the good-looking girls of El Paso. Gates enjoyed his usual status of "Director-General."

"Ladies and Gentlemen," the field announcer boomed, "The little lady you see going out to the plane with Lieutenant Sullivan is in her eighties, a pioneer of West Texas; Mrs. Martha Maynard. She has asked for a chance to fly and the Border Patrol is making an exception to its rules and will take her in one of its planes. Now, let's give this brave lady a big hand."

The several thousand spectators responded loudly. Lt. Sullivan helped the bent, silver-haired lady into the front cockpit, a bit of a task because of her billowing skirt and obvious feebleness. Then he hurried toward the crowd to reclaim his helmet.

Without warning the throaty 12 cylinders of the Liberty engine growled and then roared to a crescendo. The plane moved—accelerated—wheeled and zigged erratically across the field.

"Stop it! Stop it!" Sullivan shouted as he started in fruitless pursuit. "She must have hit the throttle!"

The plane sped faster. Women screamed. A military ambulance dashed onto the field.

Suddenly the plane's nose went up sharply. It lurched into the air—stalled—fell and hit the ground, then bounced into the air again. The little old lady's arms could be seen waving frantically.

The DeHavilland seemed to go beserk. It climbed, spiraled, dived at the field, dashed at a hangar and zoomed, missing it by inches. It roared over the cowering crowd. Finally it leveled, crossed the field, banked and came in to a slick-on landing, taxied up and stopped in front of the crowd.

"Mrs. Maynard" vaulted from the cockpit and walked up to the announcer. Somehow she was very tall, erect and vigorous. Off came a white wig. A big grin lit a homely face. This young Border Patrol pilot was a resident of a small Louisiana community north of Lake Pontchartrain. He bowed as the announcer intoned:

"You have just seen an exhibition of crazy, yet precision flying by Lt. Claire Chennault."

Chennault was already the father of seven children. Later he was to become an American legend; a general leading the famed Flying Tigers against the Japanese and still later to become president of China National Airlines.

The circus immediately appropriated the stunt and added it to its repertoire, as did scores of other barnstormers in the days to come.

One day during the week Gates and Hazel drove up in the Stevens, both crying.

"What in hell is the matter now?" Pang asked.

"R-R-Rona—our new dog," Hazel snuffled. "She's dead. Right here in the car."

The word spread rapidly to the pilots, mechanics, privates and officers of the Border Patrol. They all had played with Rona, petted her, fed her. She was a tail-wagging, affectionate animal.

Someone suggested: "We'll bury Rona with honors."

Rona was only a dog, but she had a military funeral, complete with rifle salute. A small cross was brought to mark her grave. As dirt covered the small body, Pang thought of Lou Hutt's finger.

The two men who came to the field were reserve officers, and claimed to be pilots. They demanded a plane. The line sergeant told them no DH4s were available.

Lieutenant Chennault does his act as a "little old lady" at Fort Bliss, Texas. He went on to fame as commanding general of the Flying Tigers in China.

"Can we use your airplane?" they asked Pangborn. The sergeant standing behind them wig-wagged a violent "no!"

They wandered down the line of planes, saw one that had just taxied in, and said: "We'll take this one."

The Sergeant, helpless in the face of higher rank, confided to Pang: "I don't think they can fly."

The plane taxied out to the runway, lurched into the air, climbed abruptly to fifty feet, stalled and plunged nose down. It burst into flames and was largely consumed before the fire fighters could get to it.

A crowd gathered to view the catastrophe. Pangborn felt ill, shaken. "When there's a crash, get into the air!" He climbed into his Standard, took off and put on a violent, sky-tearing exhibition of stunt flying.

"I'll get their minds away from the crash and death," he told himself.

The next day an editorial in an El Paso newspaper told of the callous, thoughtless, stupid pilot who had danced his airplane over the funeral pyre beneath him.

The increasing hassles between Gates and Yerex over contracts and money matters came to a head there in El Paso. Pangborn had likewise been irked with Yerex since their argument over the two thousand dollars. Gates came to Pang.

"Let's get rid of the guy," he said. "We'll buy him out and go it together. You've got money, haven't you?"

"Some."

An Internal Revenue accountant would have had difficulty following the involved financial adjustments which marked the split. Freddie Lund owned the parachute. Pangborn had sent $600 to Yerex to pay for a new crankshaft. Gates and Yerex were partners in the Stephens automobile used as an advance car for the circus. Yerex owed Lund $700, and finally there was another $1,600 Pang had given Yerex to buy the Standard he now claimed as his own.

The final settlement left Gates and Pangborn with the Stephens and one airplane owned jointly by Pang and Lund. After Yerex, Milt Girton, Ace the police dog, and Dewey Oster had left, Gates said:

"We've gotta have two planes for the Golden Jubilee because I've promised a plane change."

"The government has an Oriole less its K-6 engine that we can pick up for about two hundred and fifty," Pang said. "It's the one Romer Weyant once owned. You can afford it."

"Good, Pang. Now we better pick a name for our outfit. We could call it the Pangborn Flying Circus, because of your reputation and because you're putting up the money for the second plane we need. On the other hand, I've built up my name as director-general of all our shows. I think it ought to be the Gates Flying Circus."

Alien to personal vanity, Pang agreed and Gates put out his hand to shake on the deal.

"And now that we're partners, could you lend me twenty-five dollars? Hazel and I have to eat."

Years later it dawned on Pangborn that Gates had never bothered to pay his half-interest in the partnership.

The Jubilee was a financial success for the new team. Hazel was keeping the books, and Pang trusted her. He didn't ask the exact amount of the take, but estimated it as close to $3,000. Hazel was to determine profits and losses for the next several years. Always, Pang had little interest in them. He banked some money, figured he could get the remainder of his share in due time.

To replace those who had departed with Yerex, Pop Johnson and little Eddie Brooks were hired. Johnson was a Merlin with tools; a genius in keeping an OX5 grinding out its 90 horsepower. Brooks was slight, shy, reserved and looked hardly old enough to shave. However he had served as instructor of Royal Flying Corps students at Fort Worth during the war. An excellent pilot, he also had a gift for maintenance and repair.

As the show ended, Gates dipped into his mental water colors and with broad brush strokes sketched his latest inspiration.

"Pang, Denver's a hot young town. It's aviation crazy. It's a gold mine, just like the Haw Tabor diggings. We'll make a million. We'll be in on the ground floor. I hear there's only one operator in the town. We'll get those surplus planes from the Border Patrol, settle down, and start a flying school. We'll sell aviation to the Rockies with our planes going out into the high country. I've been through that territory, Pang, in the Stephens. Everybody's nuts to see an airplane, and fly. We'll be the aviation hub of the country. . ."

"Look, Van," Pang said, "don't take in too damn much territory. But. . . well, let's try it."

And so, another mountain and beyond it. . . .

11

Tie-In With Texaco

HEADING FOR DENVER, Pangborn and Gates were in the newly acquired Oriole. Eddie Brooks drove the Stephens and was accompanied by Hazel and Pop, the mechanic. On the way Pang flew over the desolate, uninhabited White Sands National Monument, which later became the test area for the government's guided missile programs.

Beyond White Sands was Raton Pass, 7,600 feet. The Hisso labored against downdrafts and headwinds while Pangborn fought the blasts which tossed them, a cork on a wild ocean of air. Finally he gave up and bounced to a landing on a flat spot beside the highway. He told Gates to take their bags and get out.

"With less weight maybe I can get across that damn pass. You flag the next bus and meet me in Trinidad."

At Trinidad, Gates's ever-seeking mind devised a new promotion. He convinced the local newspaper, *The Picketwire,* of the promotional value to be gained in dropping copies of the paper from the air. Four of the 25 copies cast overboard contained free tickets for airplane rides. Such tie-ups with local newspapers became routine with the circus and gained for it publicity far more valuable than the advertising it could not afford to buy.

In the promised land—Denver—Gates rented an abandoned sub-division near Fitzsimmons General Hospital. An office for the flying school was established in the Tabor Building downtown with Hazel in charge.

With new challenges at hand, Gates was sober and industrious for a change. He found a natural rapport with the young, vigorous men of the *Denver Post*. Gates had ideas, they had ideas, and between them the circus was built to five times its actual size. The *Post* lived on things which were new and different.

Gates tied up with everything and everybody. Broadsides in the city trollies urged people to come to the field for passenger flights and instruction. The *Post* devised new stories almost every day. For the Pageant of Progress the *Post* gave away hundreds of tickets dropped over the city in copies of the newspaper. The largess from the sky was announced by the deafening wail of a siren which had been installed on the roof of the *Post* during World War I, possibly to warn the populace in case of invasion. The promotion was so successful that the Pageant went from red to black figures.

Paul Vernier, an interior decorator, was the first student of the flying school. The charge was $25 an hour for instruction. Paul was a most apt student. Not only did he learn to fly; he became a skilled wing-walker and parachute-jumper. Later he became the first test pilot for Alexander Film Industries. J. Don Alexander, owner of the operation, had been bitten with the flying bug and decided to build airplanes. The Alexander Eaglerock was his first. It was known among pilots as the Eaglebrick because of its gliding characteristics. Nevertheless, it was a popular plane of the late '20s and brought more attention to Denver as an aviation center than did the Gates operation. The flying school folded after three months.

Despite failure of the school, Gates achieved one of the major coups of his career during the Denver stay. It was possibly the greatest tie-in in the history of barnstorming. Gates went to Will Dodge, general sales manager of The Texas Company and talked him into a relationship which was to last for six years and provide mutual profitability.

Under the agreement—it was verbal—the circus was to get free gasoline and oil in the vicinity of Denver. Later it was expanded to national scope. In exchange the circus agreed to paint all its planes "Fire Chief Red" and to carry the white star and green "T" logo.

Gates provided a letter stating that the circus used Texas Company gasoline because it was the best. The letter was used in advertisements in the newspapers of whatever cities the circus was visiting. Since car and plane used the same gasoline in those days, Texaco pumps were lined up with eager buyers after every circus performance.

As another turn of the Denver venture, Gates discovered a new source of income. He noted that a number of amateurs were standing in line to make parachute jumps. The circus had promised to pay anyone who would jump. Ever the promoter, Gates turned this into an asset by charging the jumpers rather than paying them.

Professor Ivy Baldwin, the famed balloon parachutist—all male balloon jumpers were known as "Professor"—lived in Denver. A man of nerve, and fine sense of balance, he had walked a cable across a narrow part of Fourth of July canyon, near Coeur d'Alene, Idaho. He made hundreds of jumps from gas and hot air baloons, and later added airplanes. Tall, thin, his white hair and mustache made him indeed look like a "Professor."

As Lund had taken the circus's one 'chute when he left with Yerex, Pang asked old Ivy to make them a new one. In a short time he returned with his product, an exhibition 'chute which he took out and then casually pushed back into its case.

"When are you going to pack it?" Pang asked.

"I just packed it," he replied. "I've jumped these things for years. It's all right."

Pang insisted on repacking it. He placed newspapers between the shroud folds, after being certain that the body of the 'chute was neatly arranged. When the job was finished, the Professor, who must have been well into his seventies asked:

"How's about a job for me as a wing-walker?"

It was with reluctance that Pang turned him down.

Shuttling out of Denver the Circus split into two units in order to cover more territory. At Worland, an oil field community in Wyoming, Pangborn saw one of the few alien airplanes he had encountered in the entire area. The plane was owned by Jack Lynch and it was in an arroyo near the field where the pilot had left it. A tall, very slim young wing-walker-mechanic was trying to figure out how to get the plane back on to level ground. He said his name was Lindbergh. Most people called him "Slim." Pangborn encountered Lynch and

One of the Standards in flight, showing the Texaco tie-in arranged by Van Gates.

Lindbergh again at Lewistown, Montana. Lindberg had taken eight hours of instruction at the Nebraska Aircraft Company in Lincoln, Nebraska. They told him that he should go out with a barnstormer and build up his flying time if he wanted to become a qualified pilot. Lynch was giving him stick time in exchange for his mechanical skills.

Lynch was the pilot who made aviation history when he flew day and night from Shelby, Montana to Chicago in July, 1923, with films of the Jack Dempsey-Tommy Gibbons fight. He was later killed in Arizona while flying young Cornelius Ryan of the Anaconda Copper family.

At the Cheyenne Frontier Days, Eddie scraped a hummock with the Oriole. The tip of one blade of the propeller was damaged. Pangborn suggested they saw off the five inches of the damaged end and an equal amount from the other end. This caused the engine to turn up a couple of hundred more revolutions per minute thus giving the plane greater power. It also proved that a square-end propeller was both practical and efficient. Pangborn and the crew took no advantage of their discovery. Square-blade props were seen on many military aircraft in World War II.

Never take anything but cash! Pangborn learned it the hard way; this latest lesson in his long economics education. There had been a grand week at the Corn Palace Celebration at Mitchell, South Dakota. The organization had given the circus a contract for "the works," including wing-walking, parachute-jumping, upside-down flying and night fireworks. In addition it had exclusive passenger carrying rights.

Pang was to be paid $2,000 by the fair management for the circus's performance, in addition to what was earned carrying passengers. W. H. King, Manager, asked if he wanted cash or a check.

"Two grand is too much to carry," Pang replied. "Give me five hundred in cash and the rest as a check."

He didn't cash the check at once, believing the Corn Palace committee, in view of the success of the show, to be solvent. It was. But the bank wasn't. It failed and the check bounced. Pang resolved that in the future he would take nothing but cash.

After encountering Lynch and Lindbergh in Lewistown, Pangborn set out for Idaho to visit his mother whom he had not seen for more than a year.

He was following the iron compass, in this case the tracks of the Chicago, Milwaukee, St. Paul and Pacific railway. Fog and a drizzle had forced him down almost to telegraph pole height. The railroad branched; he followed the right hand rails. In a few miles they ended abruptly as they entered a tunnel. Pang did a fast wing-over and landed in a pasture which was part of the Ringling ranch, owned by the Ringling brothers of circus fame.

A man drove up in a car.

"Got anything for me?" he asked.

Pang explained that the weather had forced him down, whereupon the man took him to the ranch house, offered him a drink and pointed to the bottle.

"This is what I expected you were bringing me," he said. "I have a bootlegger who flies my grog in from Canada regularly."

When the bad weather continued Pang took the train from Helena to St. Maries. Five years were to elapse before he would see his mother again.

The Pangborn-Gates partnership nearly came to an end in Sante Fe, New Mexico as the circus worked its way south. Tommy Thompson, Pangborn, and Geraldson had nearly frozen in a biting north wind as they tied down the planes against the threat of whipping gray clouds. In the hotel lobby they gathered within scorching distance of the crackling fire-place fire.

Gates and Hazel came into the lobby a little later. Gates saw Pang and the others warming by the fire, and with blood in his eyes, stalked over.

"Why in hell aren't you guys out flying?"

"Van," Pang replied. "You've blown a piston. It's Christmas Eve! People don't want to fly! Further, it's freezing out there in that wind."

Gates continued to berate the "softies." Pang silenced him.

"Shut up, Van. I'm tired of beating around mountain peaks, my ears blue, my nose numb. I'm going where it's warm. You can come along or stay here, it makes no difference to me."

Gates calmed a bit, but remained belligerent.

"We'll wear ourselves down to our sox in that flat country," he protested. "Hell, I read yesterday that there are more than a hundred and sixty airports now. There's a hundred and twenty-four fixed base operators. A hundred and eighty Army planes flew into St. Louis for the International air races. There's more than twenty factories turning out new crates. We'll starve!"

"Okay, so we starve!" was Pang's final word.

It was at Houston, as the circus put on the show at Ellington Field in mid-1924, that Rosalie Gordon had been rescued from almost certain death. And there, too, Duke Krantz had joined the circus.

While the show for Army Air Service was staged over Ellington Field, the circus was based on another field northwest of the city. A mystery developed when it was discovered that seven Standards had been built up in shops on the field. Pang was afraid that this was a new circus, designed to give them the toughest competition.

The manager of the operation was not talkative. A girl, in a mink coat, picked him up each evening in a Cadillac. Tommy Thompson, exercising his way with women, managed to meet the girl without trouble, but he couldn't learn anything from her. Then, adding more mystery, Freddie Lund, who had quit the circus at El Paso, appeared on the field with six other pilots. Lund, too, would not reveal what the planes were for, nor where they were going. Without fanfare the planes were cranked, took off and disappeared.

After the planes plus the manager and the mechanics who had worked on them had left, the beautiful girl stopped by the shop, picked up Thompson—and he wasn't seen for a week.

Some time later, in another part of the country, Pang met Lund who related what the mysterious operation was all about.

"One of those banana republics in Central America was due for a revolution," he explained. "The revolutionaries bought the planes and hired us. If we had gotten to where we were supposed to go, the government would have changed fast. We would have had the only planes in Central America.

"But it didn't work out. That manager fellow you saw on the field somehow learned that the G-men were after him and we left Houston in a hurry, as you know. We headed for Florida. Three of the ships had trouble before they got to the rendezvous at Ocala. Nobody met us there. We stuck around for a while and then I took the plane assigned to me and barnstormed around the state. I never saw anybody connected with the Central American operation and nobody ever questioned me about ownership of the plane. I still have it."

All the time the circus was in Houston a small, intelligent looking and very curious youth was around the airplanes constantly. He bombarded the pilots and mechanics with questions. His questions made sense and all the crew took pains to give him solid answers.

"What's your name?" Pang asked him one day.

"Benny Howard."

Benny Howard later designed and built the racing planes "Ike" and "Mike." He built "Mr. Mulligan" which crashed during a Bendix race and took one of Howard's feet with it. Before all that he had designed and built the sport biplane, the Howard DGA-1, which, he explained, stood for "damned good airplane." Howard still later became an officer and supervisor of flight testing at the Douglas Aircraft Corporation.

Tommy Thompson announced in Houston that he was quitting the circus and that he and Joe Casey were going to Salt Lake City to start a fixed base operation. Tommy later joined United Air Lines and became one of its outstanding pilots. He was on final approach to San Francisco airport one night when his microphone slipped from its hook and jammed the controls of the DC3. Tommy and fourteen passengers died in the waters of San Francisco Bay.

12

Judge and the Town Champp

CONSTANTLY ON THE MOVE from town to town, leading lonely hotel-bound lives, with no possibility of developing lasting, meaningful relationships with the girls who flitted through their lives, the men of the circus directed their pent-up affections to animal mascots. And since most boys have had a dog as pet, it was a succession of dogs that became as much a part of the circus as the mechanics and performers who came and went.

First, in the earliest days of the circus, there had been Ace, the German shepherd. He was a dutiful guardian of the one or two planes, keen judge of the intent of people who crowded about the ticket sellers, and an inquisitive overseer of the work performed in repairing a broken wing, or attaching a new propeller.

When Gates and Yerex had their show-down in Texas, Yerex, before demanding his split of the equipment and money on hand, insisted that he be permitted to take Ace with him.

Following a series of Dobermans, Collies and a Cocker or two, some of which deserted to the more quiet life of a town dog, there had been Rona. She had died of some mysterious disease and the distraught Hazel and Van had brought her to the field in Texas where she had been accorded a proper burial with military honors, including a rifle salute.

As a small boy on the ranch along the Columbia River and as a teen-ager in Idaho, Pang had always had a dog. He loved the animals first as playmates and later as hunting companions.

Here in Alamosa, Colorado, on a frosty fall afternoon when the aspens were a golden yellow and new snow dusted the higher peaks, he was walking down the street when he saw a German shepherd dog behind a fence. The dog nuzzled Pang's hand in the silent communication of man and dog. He was a beautiful animal, strong in the shoulder. The set of the head, the appraising eyes showed his intelligence.

A middle-aged man came out of the house.

"That's a fine dog you have," Pang said.

"Comes from the Sierra Blanca Kennels here. The best."

Conversation developed that the man was a local judge, and that he found that he could no longer keep the dog. He had had many offers; one of $750 from Jack Dempsey. He didn't feel, however, that from any of the offers the dog would have a real home.

"I can't give him a home either because we're on the road," Pang said. "But he will have love, and the very best care. The Gates Flying Circus needs a mascot. How about it?"

After a discussion of dogs Pang had had as a lad and his explanation of what the circus was and who they were, the man said he already knew considerable about them. Perhaps he was influenced by the instant friendship that had sprung up between the dog and Pang.

"I think he will have good care, young man. You may have him."

Judge changed owners as Pang paid the man $250.

That was how the flying police dog joined the circus. He was a companion on the ground, guardian of equipment, and playfully eager for a romp with any of the roustabouts.

Judge rode in the front cockpit between stops, on the lap of one of the wing-walkers. He loved flying, and almost seemed to be smiling. He'd bark joyfully when someone waved from another plane in the formation.

In describing Judge to a friend, Pang said he was kindly, affectionate, devoted, laughable and forgiving. "What more can you say about a dog?" he concluded.

Judge was a ham. He seemed to recognize a camera, whether in the hands of amateur or professional. Few pictures of his day show the pilots or airplanes without Judge in the foreground, ears upright, almost a smile on his muzzle.

In a letter to his mother, Pang wrote: "I am enclosing some pictures of my dog, Judge, taken some time ago. He is the center of attraction wherever we go. Mrs. Gates is taking care of him for me. I do not want to get too attached to him as I would then miss him that much more if I had to sell him."

The men of the circus were convinced that Judge considered himself a member of the crew; that he had developed superiority traits, regarding himself as above the ordinary, street-running dogs of the communities they visited. He displayed a dignity when strangers were about, in keeping with his self-esteem.

Clyde Pangborn and the flying mascot, Judge.

At Newnan, Georgia, a man followed by a large mean-looking dog of obvious cross-breeding, came up to Pang.

"My dog here is the champion of the city. You'd better keep that critter of yours away from him while you're here. Otherwise I won't be responsible for what might happen."

A couple of days later the man returned to the field, again accompanied by his dog. One of the ground crew had driven the Lincoln into town and had brought back box lunches for his busy, but hungry comrades. He'd left both rear doors open while he went to summon the others. The local canine champ sniffed, jumped into the car, and already had attacked his second box when Judge saw him.

A gray streak tore silently across the field and into the car, teeth slashing, neck-hair on end. The champion dashed out the other door, yelping, with Judge on his tail. Judge abandoned the chase only after the other dog was well on his ignominious retreat to town.

The melee had attracted the crew members and the champ's owner, all of whom came running.

"Damndest thing I ever seen, damndest thing ever," the bewildered owner muttered over and over.

Judge was well-versed in fighting tactics. Early in his career he had arrived at Murphysboro, Illinois, as usual in the cockpit of one of the planes. Several local canines, resenting the intrusion of a stranger into their territory, decided on a gang attack. Judge ran for the Lincoln, used it as a backstop to protect his rear, and picked off the local dogs one by one as each took a turn challenging—until he had sent the pack tucktailed and yelping in defeat.

Judge, alas, became the victim of prohibition. A bootlegger, seeking new customers, came snooping around the supply truck where Judge was on guard while the crew was in town. When Judge challenged the intruder, the man, in a panic, pulled a six-shooter and killed him.

Judge was buried at the edge of the flying field, close by the airplanes and the pilots with whom he had shared the sky.

13

There Goes Another Con Rod

FORCED LANDINGS, usually the result of failure of a connecting rod in the temperamental OX5 engines, were routine, but nevertheless exciting, if not lethal. They invariably occurred over wooded or very rough terrain thus testing the ingenuity of the pilots in slipping the powerless craft to a landing on a postage-stamp bit of the best available ground. The low landing speed of the Jenny—30-40 miles an hour—permitted many pilots to walk away from crashes which had demolished their planes.

Pang experienced his first forced landing on the second day that he and Reed owned their own Jenny following discharge from the Air Corps. They were flying north in California, Mt. Shasta an ice-cream sundae on their right, Black Butte at their wing-tip. Suddenly eight cylinders became seven, the oil-pressure gauge went to zero, and a teeth-rattling vibration set-up.

Get down quick! Pang knew the way. That "deadly" tailspin, only now it was simply the shortest, quickest way of getting down. The landing was to join a herd of cows in a field near Montague and in turn was to lead to the close-call romance at Yreka.

Over Portland, Oregon, an engine simply quit. No arguing, no spluttering cough, it just stopped. Pang counted his blessings as he slipped to what appeared to be a providential landing field near the fair grounds. It was a carefully maintained polo grounds. The tail skid tore the turf to ribbons. An irate caretaker stormed at Pang:

"This ain't no place to land. Planes should land on the golf course!"

After a broken magneto wire was discovered and replaced, Pang took the caretaker's advice and hopped over to the golf course which had been pointed out to him. He picked a particularly smooth, green spot on which to park his plane. Pang knew little of polo and still less of golf and its greens. Two gaffes in one day!

At Fresno Pang had removed the stick from the front cockpit while carrying passengers. When his upside-down flight was announced and he had moved to the front cockpit he jammed the stick into the socket, but in his hurry failed to put the securing pin in place. He took off, climbed, half-looped on to his back, and was gliding downward when the stick came loose in his hand. The plane labored on its back, went into uncontrolled gyrations as Pang tried to jam the tapered end of the stick back into place.

A hill was between him and the field; he was losing altitude fast. The spectators could no longer see him, and already were assuming that he had crashed. He kept jabbing the stick and at last got it in place, half-rolled just above the ground and sat down abruptly as potential, but disappointed, souvenir hunters rushed up.

Out of Salida, Colorado, Pang was headed for Palmer Lake Pass, 7,237 feet. Lloyd Geraldson, wing-walking acrobat was in the front cockpit, Tommy Thompson in a second plane behind him. Pang was following that reliable early-day compass, the railroad tracks, as fog forced him lower and lower. Ice made the windshield translucent, built up on the leading edges of the wings. The controls became sloppy. It was impossible to turn around in the narrow, wooded canyon, a situation in which all too many pilots had found themselves.

Pang could no longer see Thompson behind him. He was forced lower and lower. Twenty feet above the tracks, ten, five. The landing gear snagged a switch standard—the plane pitched, skidded, and slid into the ditch beside the tracks. The tail was in the air, extending over the rails. Tommy, following, might hit it, or a train could slice it off.

"Run south," Pang shouted to Geraldson. "Flag down Tommy and any train—if you can."

Pang dashed north along the ties for a mile or more, came to a station, gasped for breath as he tried to talk to the agent.

"Take it easy son," the man said. "Agent at the last station you passed wired you'd probably bust your machine between him and me."

Tommy had turned back before entering the canyon. The wrecked plane was trucked to Denver. Gates, fortunately in one of his better moods, had observed at the wreck site: "What the hell kind of field is this?"

It can be very disconcerting if a connecting rod lets go at the top of a loop. Particularly if it is night and your plane is spouting a golden cascade of fireworks.

Pang finished the loop. He was over pine trees and ten miles from the small field from which he had taken off at Orlando, Florida. The fireworks continued to burn, the longest burning fireworks in the history of barnstorming, while Pang played with the throttle, trying to milk enough power from the engine to get back to the field. It clattered, bucked, snorted, wheezed and finally died, along with the fireworks, just short of the field. Wire Jacuzzi for a new prop; repair the landing gear once more.

At Bartow, Florida, Pang experienced that worst of all heart-stoppers. His engine quit on take-off. Just beyond the field was a small rise, and two men in their Model T had parked behind it to watch them "gol-durned airyplanes" go overhead.

When Pang saw them it was too late. He smacked the car full on. It rolled onto its side, the occupants spewed to the ground, and the plane slewed to a dust-hidden stop. The two men ran as though pursued by the devil himself. The plane had a broken landing gear, engine mount, propeller and lower wing spar.

The next day Pang learned where the men lived and went to see them.

"How much do I owe you for the crack-up?"

"Done wrecked us purty bad," said one.

"Fifty too much?" ventured the other.

Pang whipped out a release, all barnstormers carried them, had them sign it, then said: "How'd you boys like to come out and take an airplane ride?"

"No siree! No thank you. We don't never want to even see no airyplane again."

As the oil pressure dropped to four from its normal 60 to 70 pounds, Pang told himself he should have stayed in Quincy, Illinois and overhauled the engine before heading east to Springfield.

The plane was slopping along at 4,000 feet below angry black storm clouds. Up front Duke Krantz rode with an assortment they had learned to carry in their perambulations. Included were Ford axles with which to anchor the planes in winds, engine and cockpit covers, a spare wheel, a tool box, spark plugs and other small spare parts, a couple of steel posts, gasoline and water cans, rope and their individual bags. On the lower right wing an extra propeller was lashed to the first strut.

Lightning flashed a warning ahead. They did not hear the thunder, but they did hear the crash, bang, clank as another connecting rod let go. Black smoke poured out. Duke turned and shouted: "Engine's burning up inside. Rod smashed the gas line."

No spin or dive this time. Instead Pang slipped steep, fast and into a spiral. The slip blew the flames out between the wings close to the first strut, but away from the two men in the cockpit.

As the ground grew closer, Duke was busy throwing everything from the front cockpit. Wiping his smoke-smudged goggles, Pang spotted a possible landing place; a hogback between two creek bottoms.

He had to straighten out from the slip in the last few feet. The flames shot straight back and ignited the oil-soaked fuselage. They hit and were still rolling fast when Pang shouted: "Jump, Duke!"

Duke tossed out their bags and dived. Pang went out head first, bounced and rolled down the sloping hogback into the creek. He got to his feet groggily and started after the plane which was sliding sidewise, like a baserunner stealing second. It pitched, went up on its nose and flames reached toward the black, rain-charged clouds overhead as gasoline, nitrate-doped fabric, spruce and plywood burst into flame. Just as Pang halted short of the pyre, his tumbling bag rolled near him. He raced to it, got out his camera and snapped pictures though nearly blinded by the rain. Duke grabbed him.

"Move, you idiot, before you drown."

They raced to a tree. As they got under it there was a crackling, hissing, sizzling boom overhead, and the strange smell of ozone. The bolt struck the tree and cracked a large limb. The two ran into the storm again and huddled in a ditch near the plane which offered some shelter.

Duke muttered: "On fire, deadstick landing down hill, cross wind! Lady luck sure was with us that time."

"Okay," Pang replied. "But don't forget that I was the guy at the controls."

They heard yells and shouts. Half a dozen farmers surrounded the charred skeleton. One asked:

"Where in hell's th' bodies?"

"Here we are," Pang said as the farmers swung around startled, open-mouthed. He had an idea. He handed one of the men the damp camera and asked if he would take a picture of him and Duke in front of the still smoking wreck. As they posed there was a great whoosh directly behind them, followed by a dull boom. The lower pressure tank, containing about twenty gallons of gasoline, had just blown up.

"We sure should have overhauled that engine in Quincy," Pang observed.

It had been a good week at Quincy. One eager young fellow had offered to show Pang the city after he had taken his first airplane ride. He had a car, knew plenty of girls and was familiar with the road houses and night clubs of the area.

"I'm going to learn to fly," he declared. "But I'm interested in radio too. I've studied it a lot. I think radio will mean a lot to pilots some day."

His name was Bill Lear. The company he developed, Lear Developments (now Lear-Siegler) Inc., has contributed immeasurably in the perfection of aircraft communication, homing devices, landing systems and many other applications of electronic science to aircraft operation.

14

Dames and Pilots

FROM EARLIEST DAY men of action have intrigued women. The Tuscan dolls had an eye for the Roman legionnaires, Corinthian maids were sly visitors to the Grecian army camps, Indian maids slipped from the family tepees to tryst with the warriors who carried the most scalps at their belts.

Aviators! Pilots! Barnstormers! They had a magnetic attraction for the feminine sex as positive as north for the compass needle. The pilots themselves created part of the mystique. They dressed in fancy twill trousers, tight at the calf, flaring at the knee. They wore high-polished boots of Cordovan leather, silk scarves about the neck, goggles raised to leather helmets. They had perfected the art of sweet-talk and could make the most ordinary looking girl believe she was an irresistible siren. Most of them were single, thus highly eligible.

"Lend me five bucks, Pang," big Jack Ashcraft pleaded one hot, humid summer evening in Florida. "This dame is picking me up, and I gotta buy some hootch."

The next morning a red-eyed, sleepy-looking Jack reported to Pangborn.

"Damndest thing, Pang. That gal drove up in this big roadster, and she had on a fur coat! In this weather! Ninety-five degrees! I thought she was nuts! You won't believe this, Pang, but I later discovered she didn't have a damn thing on under that coat!"

One day Tommy Thompson told Pang he was going to fly over to Post, Texas, where he had left some pedigree chickens in care of a rancher. Pang asked where he could pick up a few quick bucks while Tommy was away.

"Crosbyton," Tommy replied. "It's hot! I really cleaned up there."

He paused, rubbed the toe of his boot in the ground.

"But there's one thing. When you land, a pretty little brunette will come out to the field. She's a Sunday School teacher and very proper. Be careful of your language."

Tommy was right. Shortly after Pang landed, the girl appeared with a very attractive companion. In their presence Pang was so considerate and careful of his language that he too could have qualified for a Sunday School job. Just as he was about to take off to return to base, the charming teacher said:

"Give my love to Tommy. By the way, where is he?"

"I think he's over at Post. He told me he wanted to check on some chickens he left there last year."

"Chickens, hell!" the brunette exclaimed. "They're girls, and that guy'll knock 'em up!"

When Pang bawled out Tommy for his two-way deception, Tommy replied:

"Pang, it's perfectly all right to use my field, carry passengers out of my town, but dammit, I've got a right to hang onto my own women."

It was then that Tommy told Pang about the time he'd had a forced landing in a remote area. He flagged down a passenger train and climbed aboard in his flight regalia; helmet, goggles, boots and leather coat. He went to the smoker where a very large, ham-fisted and obviously unhappy man started a conversation.

"You're a flier, I see. Can you tell me where I can find a pilot named Tommy Thompson?"

"I dunno . . .," Tommy hedged. "Why?"

"Well, he got a girl in trouble, and the girl blamed it on me. I had to pay. If I find that son-of-a-bitch, I'll kill him with my bare hands."

"Never heard of the dirty bum," Tommy replied.

He got off the train at the next stop, and waited five hours for a following train. Those large hands had looked extremely ominous.

Small towns produce some of the nation's cutest girls and this one was a winner. She had flown with Pang in the afternoon and a date

Tommy Thompson, who had a way with women.

had been arranged for the evening. After a picture show, the principal amusement offered in the community, they found their way to a bench in a remote, darkened corner of the city park. Pang found the girl cooperative when a noise interrupted and he saw two furtive figures lurking behind a thick bush. He took out his wallet, which contained about $1,200, unstrapped his wrist watch and dropped both into his boot.

"Why did you do that?" the girl asked.

"Looks like we're about to be robbed," Pang replied.

"Oh don't worry. Them's just two of my farmer boy friends. They want to see how far I'll go."

The wages of sin, and the troubles that could befall a barnstormer were brought out with extreme clarity when the driver of the supply truck picked up a willing girl, the daughter of a Virginia farmer. When the circus landed at Frederick, Maryland, a man wearing a large star on his chest asked if there was a pilot named "X" in the outfit.

As a matter of course anyone working with the circus represented himself as a pilot when in an exploratory conversation with a girl. Pang answered that "X" was the supply truck driver.

"I'm the constabule," the man with the star said. "Seems like this here gal's pappy is purty mad on account this boy took that girl over a state line. Her and her pappy won't make no fuss if this boy'll marry her."

The young man, when ramifications of the Mann Act were explained to him, said he would be happy to marry the girl. Pang sent Duke Krantz in to Frederick to give the bride away.

"Seemed sort of silly," Duke said when he returned from the ceremony. "She'd already given herself away."

Many of the fliers played their role of Don Juan with the aplomb of a Barrymore. None was more flamboyant, more dashing, than Roscoe Turner, who called himself Colonel. His breeches were pink, a Sam Browne belt slashed across his carefully tailored tunic. On occasion he wore a cerise-lined cape. A Doberman with perpetual snarl completed his working ensemble.

Turner, billing himself as "The World's Greatest Aviator," was appearing at a theatre in the same town as the circus. Pang and Mickey Efferson went to catch his act.

"Often my dog here and I go aloft in one of my airplanes and I invent stunts," Turner told his enraptured audience, largely female. "These are spectacular tricks which I willingly pass on to others. For instance, I developed and presented to the flying circus that's here some of its most thrilling spectacles."

Pang had to restrain Mickey from going up over the footlights.

The next day Mickey was refueling one of the planes on the field when a huge, open touring car rolled up. In it were Roscoe, the dog and not one, but two, gorgeous gals.

"And these," Roscoe said as he waved an all-inclusive arm, "are some of my airplanes!"

Mickey drew up to his full height and said, "You're a goddamn liar, Turner. These planes belong to the Gates Flying Circus."

Roscoe's flush of crimson challenged that of his cape's lining. Years later Pang recalled the incident to Turner. Roscoe smiled politely, but he was not amused.

Jack Ashcraft had been playing house with a married woman at

Bradenton. Pang didn't know Jack had written her advising that he was at St. Petersburg, and suggesting that she come over there.

She showed up. A short time later her husband, a small, bland type of shy mien, approached Pang.

"I think my wife is visiting the circus. Is Mr. Ashcraft here?"

"That's Ashcraft over there," Pang pointed.

He saw the two men in earnest conversation. Finally the visitor left. Jack, breathing heavily and obviously agitated, staggered over to Pang.

"That guy was carrying the biggest gun I've ever seen bulging a man's pocket. But I talked him out of using it. Let's have a snort!"

The potato deal in Idaho was only one of the trades Pang had been tendered over the years. People had offered fruit, turkeys and chickens, eggs by the crate in exchange for an airplane ride. All such offers were topped, however, when a good-looking, well-dressed, but overly made-up woman drove up in an Apperson Jackrabbit roadster while the circus was working a small community.

"I run the local house, the only one in town," she told Pang. "My girls would love to take a ride with your pilots. How about an even-up trade?"

Pang declared his strictly cash policy.

There were exceptions, of course, to the love 'em and leave 'em policy of most pilots. Eddie Brooks fell in love with a girl in Rock Springs, Wyoming—Nelle Wulfolk, secretary of a mining company. Whenever the circus was within three hundred miles of Rock Springs, Eddie would borrow a plane and head straight for the Wyoming town. Eventually he married the girl.

Then there was Pangborn's narrow escape from matrimony at Yreka, and its bonus offer of a Rolls Royce, European honeymoon and a 10,000 acre ranch.

Pang had opted to play the field. There was the daughter of a Houston oil man who followed Pang to Denver on the pretext that she was entering college there. They broke up in Cheyenne. In his address book could be found Mildred, Winnie, Margery, Nancy, Kiki, Gloria, Hope, June, Laura. . . .

15

Six Men Swing

IT WAS TO BE the largest mass hanging in the history of Louisiana. Six men, convicted murderers and bank robbers, were to be hanged behind a moat and stockade at Amite, Louisiana, 90 miles northwest of New Orleans. State troopers were to be posted outside and no one, including newspaper men, was to be allowed to witness the event. This, authorities explained, was because the men had many friends and there were rumors that a mob might attack the stockade in an attempt to free the prisoners.

Gates went to the New Orleans *Item,* an afternoon daily, and proposed to take aerial photographs of the hanging. The editors were enthusiastic; in fact, offered to pay $100 for a usable picture.

Through connections the *Item* determined the time set for the executions. Pangborn took off for Amite as the fateful hour neared, with Gates in the rear cockpit holding a huge press camera provided by the *Item*. Cruising at low altitude above the stockade Pang could see that two scaffolds were being used, the half-dozen condemned men apparently being dropped in pairs. Two were already gone by the time he had analyzed the procedure. Then he circled, dived and banked over sharply, and Gates snapped his shutter on the last pair just as the traps opened.

Pang pulled out of the vertical bank at less than 50 feet over the stockade, pushed the throttle to the firewall and sped to the Peters Avenue field. There a motorcycle rider picked up the exposed plate and rushed it to the *Item*. Less than three hours later the *Item's* front page was covered with the one-in-a-million, sharp-focus, sensational picture of the men dropping to their death.

The *Item* had given Gates and Pangborn rights to the negative outside New Orleans. Pictures were sold to numerous publications throughout the country, clearing more than a thousand dollars net.

As a result of the sensational success of the hanging picture Gates found the *Item* as responsive to his wild ideas as was the *Post* in Denver. In fact, its enterprising editors helped in devising new stunts—such as aerial marriages. With the Standards converted to carry four passengers, plus the pilot, they were able to carry the bride and bridegroom, the minister and one witness. The pilot acted as the second witness.

Gates made tie-ins with various merchants who, for the publicity, would provide presents for the happy couple. The marriage caper became a regular feature of the circus. It was never difficult to find a couple willing to make their marriage vows some three throusand feet in the air.

Conversion of the Standards had been Pang's idea. When they had first arrived in New Orleans he had said to Gates: "We ought to be pretty well heeled."

"Not so well," Gates replied. "Think, Pang. Clev cracked up at St. Louis; a total wash-out. You burned one up outside Quincy. We bought the Jenny Canuck to trade in on one replacement Standard. We had to buy another, and we didn't get the Lincoln out of a box of Cracker Jacks."

"I have an idea I've been thinking about for some time," Pang said. "We've got to overhaul everything. While we're doing it why don't we make all the Standards four-place?"

"How you going to do it?"

"We'll put all the fuel tanks in the upper center wing sections. That'll give us gravity feed. We'll be rid of the pressure system. Then I'll run ash braces along the longerons from rear cockpit forward. Lock 'em with U-bolts. Jerk the front cockpit cowlings and put in plywood seats holding two people facing to the rear. We'll haul double our present payload."

"Makes sense. Go ahead and do it."

The *Item* people and Gates came up with a startling new contest.

Each day at noon Pang would fly over the *Item* building at a different altitude. Citizens were to guess that height and the five closest estimates would win tickets for airplane rides.

At first the winners came from all parts of the city. Then, mysteriously, the field narrowed to the vicinity of Tulane University. The *Item* maintained that someone in the circus crew was tipping off friends at the college. Investigation revealed that a group of engineering students had established a base line between Tulane and the Item. Using two theodolites they were able to triangulate the correct altitude. The stunt went out the window.

On election night one of the planes was rigged with red, green, yellow and white lights, each color representing one of the local candidates in a hard-fought municipal campaign. The *Item* announced that the plane would fly over the city each hour after the polls closed, with the color code to show which candidate was ahead. Pang flew the plane and brought news of victory to one candidate, of defeat to three others.

As Pang and Duke Krantz landed one day at Peters Avenue they noticed two wide, deeply-cut ruts along the dirt runway.

"Looks like a big one came in here," Duke observed.

"That's easy," Pang replied. "Erik Nelson's 'New Orleans,' one of four Army 'round-the-world' planes led by Lowell Smith. After they finished the flight where they had started in Seattle, each plane went to the city for which it was named. Smith, flying 'Miss Chicago' was given ten thousand dollars and a Packard automobile by the Windy City community leaders. The people of New Orleans gave Erik a twenty-five dollar silver cup."

"Think of it. Clear around the world. Makes us look like amateurs," Duke mused.

"We'll all be doing it some day," Pang observed. "Look at the improvements in the last few years. There's regular day and night mail service between New York and San Francisco. Remember? It was only three years ago that Jack Knight flew from North Platte to Chicago at night following those bonfires."

"And Tony Fokker's starting to build closed-cabin jobs up there at Teterboro,"Duke added. "Sure as hell that means airlines."

Look, Duke, there's something else that makes me wonder how

long we are going to last. There's a lot of talk that Congress may set up a Bureau of Aeronautics in the Department of Commerce before long. I wonder what that will do to us?"

Two new pilots joined the circus in New Orleans, William S. (Bill) Brock and Jack Ashcraft. Brock had been working with Jerry Ringle, Burly Burns and Mabel Cody.

"I'm Ashcraft—Jack Ashcraft," the leaner of the two introduced himself. "I've been flying over Texarkana way with Buck Steele. Mebbe you've heard?"

"I haven't heard," Pang replied. "But can you splice a wing?" He pointed to the striped wing of the Standard behind him.

"Sure can."

Pang left for lunch in town and to run various errands. He returned in mid-afternoon. Ashcraft was leaning against the plane, bantering with one of the crew members.

"Dammit, I thought you were going to splice that wing!"

"So I did."

Pang went to the wing and looked at the job. It was so neat that the joint could hardly be detected. Nobody could have done the job that fast and that well, but there it was.

Ashcraft had been a motorcycle courier, a sergeant in the Army during World War I. He had managed a few hours of flying here and there since leaving the service. Pangborn found him adequate on his flight test, but a bit ragged. However, he learned rapidly.

The pilot whom Ashcraft replaced became co-pilot for the famed man-about-town Henry T. (Dick) Merrill. Merrill later made headlines by flying Harry Richmond, the entertainer, on a round-trip across the Atlantic, the wings of their plane filled with ping-pong balls to provide flotation should they be forced down at sea.

It was in New Orleans that Gates met a man who could challenge his wildest exaggerations. Gates was so impressed that he hired the word magician, along with another newspaper man; the two to act as advance men for the circus.

The man who could make the impossible sound plausible was George Alden Bruce, a reporter for the *Item*. The other was George Daws, an eager young writer who had the same hobbies as Gates—liquor and women, in either order. Bruce's first job was to produce a brochure, a 24-page color opus in which his imagination conjured impossible feats for the circus's crew. He was not reticent in listing his own achievements.

Bruce, apparently to impress hotel managers, would send letters addressed to "Prince Boris Ivanoff" to hotels in cities where the circus had been booked. On arrival he would call for his mail in the name of both George Alden Bruce and Prince Ivanoff. He would then explain that he was a Russian prince traveling incognito, and ask the hotel operator to keep his secret.

Dawes, the other advance man, had little respect for pilots or airplanes.

"Those damn pilots read the crud I get into the newspapers about them and they start to believe it. They aren't fit to live with. The only time I give a damn about an airplane is when it's flying around a field—fully loaded. That means I've got a 10 per cent commission coming."

Bill Brock, flying out into the countryside thought he had found the mother lode. Below he saw a beautiful spot on which to land. He glided down to a perfect three-pointer on one of the finest fields the piney, bayou-rift, swamp country had to offer. Neat, attractive buildings formed a symmetrical pattern nearby. People rushed to the plane.

"This is swell," Bill thought. "Good field, lots of people and they all look eager to fly."

Then he asked, "Where am I? What are all these buildings?"

"The United States Leprosarium at Carville, Louisiana," one of the spectators replied, then added: "We're lepers. We have leprosy."

Brock had the common, but erroneous, belief that the disease is highly contagious. Gunning the engine and nearly bowling over the assembled group, he made a fast, downwind take-off, abandoning his potential gold-mine.

A new twist was added to the circus's stunts by a youth named Walker. He would seemingly be hanging by his teeth at the end of a wire below the spreader bar of Bill Brock's plane as it flew down broad Canal Street. For this trick Walker wore an invisible harness under his arm pits, attached to another wire also fastened to the spreader bar. May would have scoffed at such sissy precaution.

Pangborn had advised Brock: "If Walker gets hung up, fly down to the seaplane ramp and dump him in the river. Somebody's always there and they'll fish him out."

Walker went into his act down the length of the street, and kept on hanging when he should have pulled himself back up to the plane. Brock could feel his struggling, like a fish on the end of a line. He took him out over the water, low, and along side a tug. He made four passes by the tug and close to the seaplane ramp before Walker finally let go. Brock saw the splash, and a rowboat rush out with three men in it. One of the men dived repeatedly into the muddy river. Each time he came up empty-handed.

The circus posted a $1,000 reward, but Walker's body was never found.

16

Luck—All Bad

BARNSTORMING PILOTS generally were a superstitious lot. They knocked on wood. They carried dolls and other good luck charms in their planes. Some, operating in the deep south, were even suspected of bringing voodoo down on their rivals.

Even Pang believed in luck, and right now it was all bad. Jack Ashcraft had taken a couple of fares for a stunt flight. He gave them a few loops, a whip stall and wound up with a voluntary spin. He failed to check the spin and augered in. One boy was dead. It was the first passenger fatality the circus had ever suffered and already it had flown more than one hundred thousand passengers. The other youth and Jack each had broken arms. Jack couldn't explain what had happened.

Fearful of lawsuits and attachments, the partners decided they must get all their equipment out of Louisiana. Since Jack couldn't fly, Pang hired a downy-cheeked youth to take one of the planes out of New Orleans. After a quick check flight Pang sent him on his way.

"Fly out east. You'll pick up two railroads, one going northeast across Lake Pontchartrain and one going due east, toward Mobile. Don't take the line across the lake into Slidell."

So, of course, that's what the youngster did. He finally realized his mistake and turned south toward the right railroad and the gulf. But he was running out of fuel. The Standard he was flying was the only plane not yet converted to the four-passenger configuration. It still had the center tank above and the pressure tank below. He hadn't turned off the pressure pump. It was sending the fuel in the lower tank into the upper, and out the vent.

Near Logtown, Mississippi, the empty carburetor sucked at the last drops of fuel. The pilot dead-sticked into a stump-filled patch of marshland. He wasn't hurt, but it took several days to mend the plane. Jack Ashcraft volunteered to do it despite his broken arm.

With these arrangements completed Pang flew into the Peters Avenue field to pick up Gates who was waiting with his camera and sundry personal belongings. Pang made his usual beautiful landing, but as he rolled out on the runway the landing gear collapsed.

"Aviation ain't practical," Gates stormed. "I'm going to take all this stuff to the station and get a train to Montgomery. I'll see you there."

Meantime, Bill Brock up at Brewton, flying a couple of girls, snagged a wing on a tree and ground-looped violently. One girl had a broken arm, the other was bruised, and Bill narrowly missed losing an eye when he hit the panel. Only the L-6 engine was salvagable from the wreck.

Finally what was left of the clan gathered at Montgomery where they had a commitment with the *Advertiser*. Even then, bad luck still pursued. Ashcraft, ever willing to help, cranked Brock's engine despite his broken arm. He lost his balance, spun around and the prop smacked his left leg. As a result he had a crutch to go along with the sling supporting his arm.

A short time later Brock said:

"Pang, I think I'll cash out. I've got other plans."

His account was settled. Brock headed north to fly the mail. Later, flying a Stinson Detroiter, one of the new cabin monoplanes, he and William F. Schlee, Detroit oilman, flew from Newfoundland to Japan via Europe and Asia—12,295 miles. The barrier of the then unflyable Pacific Ocean stopped them in Tokyo. The following year they set a 59-hour duration flight record at Rockwell Field, San Diego.

Bad luck still trailed the circus, darting in now and then to land a telling, and expensive blow. It was the usual field, hot and dusty, with a few customers straggling out for rides. The Texas Company man, not knowing where the fuel drums were wanted, had left them in the middle of the field. Pang had sent a roustabout and several of the kids, who invariably hung about, to roll the drums over to the bull pen. They had just started to work when "Whispering Bill" Brooks floated in, his mind doubtlessly on the blonde of the night before. The roustabout and the kids scattered. The Standard made a perfect three-point landing on the drums and disintegrated. Luck relented to the extent that no one was hurt.

"Half a county to land in and you pick on the only obstacles for miles," Pangborn exploded. "You've just flown yourself out of an airplane and a job."

"Now look, Pang, you guys are wrong. You shouldn't have them drums out in the middle of the field."

"We won't get anywhere arguing, Bill. I said you're through. We can't have anybody that dumb flying for us. You might have killed one of those kids."

"I'll sue you, you owe me six hundred dollars!"

Brooks followed through on the threat. The judge ruled in his favor and Gates paid off.

"No hard feelings?" Gates asked.

"Hell no. I got me a great job. Solid gold pay off. Me and another guy, Lee Mason, are going to Central America. Seems there's another revolution down there and they want pilots."

Fortune's frown seemed to turn to a smile with the signing of Al MacLatchie, his brother Jim, and a helper as concessionaire for the circus. They served hot dogs, hamburgers, coffee and soft drinks from a big tent which was hauled in a truck along with stoves, heaters and other equipment.

MacLatchie's addition was a real boon. He helped hold the crowds which came to the fields by feeding them and tending to their thirst. He served lunches to the circus crew, saving the time of a trip into town. And for all this he paid a percentage of his gross.

The ground equipment of the circus, which included the cars of the advance men, was now augmented with a supply truck. It carried a tent in which the mechanics could work protected from the weather and where a roustabout could sleep and guard the equipment. The truck was painted the same as the planes—fire chief red and brilliant green. A crowning touch was added by Leo (Red) Murphy, his flaming red hair a challenge to the red of the truck he drove and from which he gave his spiels to the crowds. Painted on the sides of the truck was a modest affirmation of the troupe's self-regard: *"World's Greatest Exhibition Aviators."*

The circus had a standard procedure whenever it moved into a new community. First the advance man would rent a field, not too far from the town itself, easily accessible by road. The trucks would arrive in advance of the planes making the trip from the last stand by night.

With MacLatchie's concession tent set up, iron fence posts would be driven into the ground near the entrance to the field. The posts would be connected by ropes to keep the crowds back. A narrow opening permitted entry for those buying rides. The area where the planes loaded was known as the "bull pen."

Murphy, after his spiel, would act as ticket seller. The pilots collected the tickets and used them in establishing their share of the take. When the crowds were large and business good, the engines of the planes would not be stopped as the pilots wheeled up to the bull pen. Passengers would be unloaded from the left side while others were being loaded on the right. Time on the ground was lost time. Keep 'em in the air.

If business lagged, or the flow from the community was slow, Pang would take off and put on his stunt routine. The parachute jump, heavily advertised, would be delayed until very late in the day in order to hold the crowd as long as possible and give them time to muster the courage to risk flight.

Occasionally a competitor, usually a local fixed-base operator would challenge "the world's greatest fliers" in a dispute over flying rights—like crows defending their carefully delineated territory.

At Coatesville, Pennsylvania, Gates made a tie-in with the Elks Lodge, but the local operator wouldn't permit use of his field. The circus moved to a field in front of the Elk's club house and started operations.

The local operator, with whom Parker D. (Shorty) Cramer was flying, moved to an adjacent field to capitalize on the crowds attracted by the circus's publicity and exploitation.

"I don't think he knows how to fly too well," Pangborn said to Ashcraft. "He's chiseling in on our crowds. The next time he takes off with a load we should be carrying, we'll keep him in the air."

"Got it," Jack grinned.

They took off. Every time the interloper tried to land they cut him off. They flew over him, beside him and around him. He was a confused, bewildered and jittery fellow when they finally let him land.

He called the sheriff, who happened to be an Elk. When Pang explained the situation to the officer, the local was ordered to stop chiseling on the club-backed show.

The evening of September 3rd was humid and sticky hot. Pang could sense an impending storm as little swirls of dust jigged along the runway. He had the planes tied down and was about to go into town when two women drove up and asked for a ride. They explained that they were school teachers and had driven a considerable distance. Pang reluctantly agreed to take them up.

He was circling the field for altitude when he saw what looked like a balloon. He headed for it and soon realized that it was an enormous airship; a huge, silver tube, rolling gently as it headed toward a darkening western sky.

Closer, he read on its side: "SHENANDOAH."

Pang swung parallel to the sleek craft. Officers in the control cabin, forward under the nose of the ship, signalled him closer and he flew for several minutes, an insignificant minnow beneath this great whale.

As it grew darker, Pang and his passengers waved goodbye. On landing the teachers thanked Pang for what they said was a thrilling experience they would never forget.

The next morning Pangborn picked up a newspaper. Huge headlines shouted: SHENANDOAH CRASHES. Pang and the school teachers had been the last to see the Shenandoah alive. Shortly after they had turned back the huge dirigible had plunged into a vicious line squall near Ava, Ohio. The violent sheer of the competing forces of air had broken the back of the great ship and her aft section plummeted to earth. Fourteen men died, including the ship's captain, Commander Zachary Lansdowne. Two others were injured. The rest of the crew free-ballooned in the bow of the ship to a safe landing, thanks to the skill of Lieutenant-Commander Charles Rosendahl. This, and the wreck of the Akron, spelled the end of the dirigible era.

Gates and Daws had gone on to Washington, D. C. to arrange for an air show at Bolling Field, proceeds of which were to go to the officers mess. Gates wired Pang to join him and the two went to visit Major H. H. (Hap) Arnold, their old friend from San Francisco days.

"Those were wonderful days at Crissy and the Marina," Pangborn remarked. "Lots of fun."

"They were quiet days," Arnold replied.

Pang sensed a sadness in the tired face.

"This Washington is a madhouse. I guess you've been reading about General Billy Mitchell's fight for a separate air force and enough money to build a suitable defense. The general has talked out of turn, and there is going to be trouble.

"But, dammit, he's right and no matter what happens, his ideas are going to be adopted. Of course, somebody will get hurt. Someone always gets hurt before they do anything in a brawl like this."

Arnold leaned back in his chair and smiled wistfully.

"Well, I shouldn't load you with my grief. You fellows have done a great job. You may not realize it, but the shows you've staged for us have done wonders in keeping flying alive while we've been forced to wear out old engines and airplanes and live off scraps thrown out the back door. Your tours around the country have helped make people understand our need for appropriations to keep going, and our need to be more than a step-child of the Army and a bunch of deadheads who are still buying horses for the cavalry."

He paused.

"To heck with it. At any rate, we're going ahead. The Army Air Service has shown Americans that an airplane can cross the continent in a single day."

Gates snorted, a laugh squinting his eyes.

"What's the fun, Van?" Arnold asked.

"That's a little faster than us, Hap," he replied. "Took Pang and me five years to make it."

Gates's publicity build up for the show at Bolling Field misfired. It was so effective that it came to the attention of the top officers of the Air Service, the superiors of Major Arnold who was sponsoring the show.

The commanding general ordered that the proceeds were to go to the corps area hospital fund, and ordered the commander of Bolling Field to assist in every way possible. With the anticipated funds diverted from their Bolling mess fund, the Field personnel lost interest.

When the show opened the hangar doors remained closed on all the Army planes. The show consisted of the four airplanes and the pilots of the Gates Flying Circus, three bombers from Langley Field, and a fourth bomber, used in a demonstration of smoke screen laying.

In the build-up for the show Pang had flown over downtown

Washington, dropping a part of the 200,000 circulars advertising the show. Along the mall he looked down on the forming of a parade by thousands of members of the Ku Klux Klan who were holding their national convention in the capital city. It occurred to him that an irresponsible mob like that, if armed, could seriously threaten the government.

A crowd of more than 100,000 turned out for the Bolling Field show. The four circus pilots outdid themselves in their efforts to make their four planes appear to be a dozen.

Duke Krantz furnished the one incident of the event. He insisted on jumping with a battered, torn exhibition 'chute. The officer of the day told him he couldn't use it. Krantz, with stubborness typical of a Swede, insisted he would. The officer compromised by agreeing that Krantz would also wear a military breast pack which he would provide.

Pangborn jumped Krantz, who slipped his 'chute so that he landed in the Potomac River which adjoins Bolling Field. The Army's breast pack was thoroughly soaked and would have to be dried carefully and then repacked. Duke would never admit that he went into the river deliberately.

''You know I wouldn't get the Army's little old 'chute wet. I just went into the river because it was softer than the field.''

Possibly to celebrate having ''made it'' to Washington, Gates, with advance man Daws, had thrown a classic drunk. Pangborn found Van at the roof garden of a Washington hotel, in company with Captain H. H. Halverson, Arnold's aide, who was cold sober and obviously embarrassed at Gates's loud mouth and the four letter words it uttered.

Pang sat down with them.

''Gotta lotta entertainin' to do here,'' Gates mumbled. ''Mus' spen' money on brass. You know, gotta be big stuff. Newspape' men too. All a buncha drunks.''

''Come on, Van,'' Pang coaxed. ''Let's get the hell out of here. We'll go some place else.''

''Hazel sent ya. Thass it. Hazel sent ya. You're spying on me, thass what.''

Pang made a mistake. He reached for the bottle on the table.

''Goddamn you, Pang, put that bottle down!''

''I just want you to stop drinking.''

"I stop when I goddamn please. You touch that goddamn bottle again and I'll throw you off this roof."

"Try it and you'll go with me."

"Great partner you've got there," Halverson said when they had finally quieted Gates and lured him off to his hotel.

17

Short Snorter No. 1

THOUSANDS OF FORMER pilots, generals, heads of state, entertainers, and civilian war workers retain among their most cherished mementos their "short snorters." A short snorter is a paper bill of any denomination and of issuance by any country, on which were inscribed the signatures of various celebrities, comrades and dignitaries. At first a short snorter was supposed to be visible proof that one had crossed an ocean or the equator, or had taken part in some memorable event. In later stages they came to represent almost anything.

It was Jack Ashcraft who originated the short snorter bit, way back in 1926. The idea expressed Jack's contriteness for a slip into one of his frequent booze-girl errors.

What was the intrigue of this short snorter business? How did it work? The protocol was simple. You challenged a man to show his short snorter. If he didn't have one, and was new to the game, you said:

"Okay, give me two bills."

You signed one of the bills and handed it back to him. You kept the other and you were at least a dollar to the good. He was now a "short snorter" and had the privilege of challenging anyone he met.

If the person you challenged already had his short snorter, you each autographed the other's. If the one challenged was a known "short snorter," but didn't have his bill on him, he had to buy you a drink. A short snorter became almost as essential as an ID card.

Back to Ashcraft. In the circus it was no secret that Jack was not

Jack Ashcraft, who originated the "Short Snorter" in 1923. He was killed while attempting an endurance flight record with the night-club hostess Viola Gentry.

averse to taking a drink, which he invariably referred to as a "short snort." When he was to awaken a member of the flying troupe, he would grab a big toe and say: "Come on, short snorter, get going."

The circus had been booked into Syracuse, N. Y., where it had an unusually successful run. The newspapers were generous in coverage. Municipal officials extended all possible cooperation and the crowds were large. Gates decided that reciprocation was in order. Taking Pang aside he said:

"The boys have been so good to us we've got to throw a champagne party; the biggest, wettest, champagne party in history. We can get all the stuff we want at Hammondsport. There's a winery down there, and we've got an inside track. (This was during the prohibition era.) We'll send Buck and Jack to bring back two plane loads."

The two took off on their mission. Buck returned late in the afternoon. Ashcraft—who had promoted a bit of personal entertainment—didn't return until the next day. When he did, Pangborn was prepared to eat him out as the tardy flier stepped from the cockpit of his plane. Ashcraft beat him to the first word.

"I've got something for you, Pang. I been thinking about it all the way down here. Gimme two bucks."

Pang fished out two of the old, large-size dollar bills. Ashcraft took them, signed his name and printed "Short Snorter No. II" on one and handed it back to the puzzled Pangborn.

"Now you're a short snorter," Jack said. "Sign your name to mine."

"Ain't that a cute gag?" Ashcraft continued. "Now we're both 'Short Snorters.' I thought it up flying up here with the fizz water. I'm letting you in first so you can start cleaning up. You make a buck a throw."

Pangborn made six or seven dollars on the deal at the big Syracuse champagne party, while Jack cashed in for much more. The gag spread among the personnel of the circus and then on to others in the flying fraternity, none of whom was averse to the easy money.

After Jack was killed, Okey Bevins gathered Jack's personal belongings, and among them found the short snorter bill number one with Pang's name on it. He gave it to Pang who retained it as one of his most treasured possessions.

For years a story circulated that the famous "organization" had been started by the renown bush pilot Joe Crosson. Crosson, during a meeting of the Quiet Birdmen in New York asked Pang:

"What's the low down on this 'short snorter' deal? I hear you know something about it. There've been some stories going around that I invented it up in Alaska."

Pang explained to Crosson the genesis of the gag.

Eventually it reached proportions that would have astounded

Reputed to be the longest "Short Snorter" in the world, this 20-footer was assembled by a Seattle photographer.

Ashcraft. It is believed that the champion short snorter is that possessed by a Seattle newspaper photographer. It is made up of more than forty bills of various denominations, each covered with signatures. It is twenty-two feet long!

After the Syracuse success Pang and the crew took time off to take in the National Air Races at Mitchel Field, Long Island. What they saw there—the new planes—startled them. They had dragged in to a landing, scarcely moving, against a strong head wind. And here was Lieutenant Cyrus Bettis winning the Pulitzer Trophy race with a speed of 248 miles an hour!

At Albany, N. Y., Gates arranged a tie-in with the *Times Union,* owned by William Randolph Hearst. George Hearst, one of the sons, and an official of the newspaper, asked if anyone would fly him to New York City. Pangborn volunteered. When they landed at Roosevelt Field, Hearst very casually peeled the $200 fee from a husky roll of bills.

There were other unusual charter jobs at Albany. One day a New York cotton broker rushed onto the field with an urgent appeal. His two children had been killed in an accident and his wife was cruising up the Hudson on the family yacht, somewhere in the vicinity of Newbergh. "Will you help me find her?" pleaded the distraught parent. "I must let her know."

Pang got a long piece of twine, put a weight on it, and fastened the message to it. The message told the wife of the tragedy and directed her to return to New York. They took off, flew down low over the river, located the boat, and lowered the message to the deck.

The wife grabbed the note and dashed below deck. Immediately the boat turned around and started down river. Pang flew the broker on to New York City. There he collected another $200 fee.

18

Gates and a "45"

GATES HAD TAKEN OFF on one of his "drunks" of increasing frequency. No one knew what thoughts his benumbed brain developed in these periods except that they were invariably malicious and venomous. They found their expression in beatings of the overly-tolerant, ever-loving Hazel, in insults directed at patrons of the circus, in destruction of property—his own and that of others.

Here in Easton, on the banks of the Delaware, Daws (the advance man) had joined Gates in the favorite pastime of both. Meanwhile, Pangborn was at the field digging in and tying down the planes for what threatened to be a severe storm. Heavy ropes were double-anchored to metal fence posts, driven deep into the earth, as rain sheeted before the wind.

Finally the job was completed and Pang, cold, wet, and weary, drove back to the hotel. As he entered the lobby he saw Mickey Efferson slumped in a chair and obviously crying.

"What's the matter?"

"Gates. . . Gates fired me, Pang."

"Forget it kid. Gates can't fire anybody who's working for me. Be on the job in the morning."

Pang then went to the desk for his key. The clerk was small, bent and aged. He too was wet-eyed and had a vivid welt across his cheek.

"And what's with you?" Pang asked.

"That Mr. Daws—he slapped me."

"Why?"

"I dunno."

John W. Underwood photo collection.

Hazel and Ivan Gates (in white shirt). Freddie Lund is seated in the auto.

"What in hell is going on?" Pang asked himself as he took the elevator. At his knock Gates opened the door of his room. The bed was covered with paper money, the day's receipts; about $1,500. Hazel was sorting and counting the money into piles in preparation for paying off the pilots and ground crew. Judge, the mascot, was drowsing on the floor. To the right of the bed were two suitcases. A washbasin was against the wall. To the left was the bathroom; an old-fashioned tub, on its hawk-talon legs, could be seen through the door.

"Come in," Gates said as Pang took two or three steps forward. Gates went behind Pang; closed the door.

"What goes on around this dump," Pang demanded. "Mickey is bawling downstairs, says you. . ."

Gates swung from behind with a wild, looping blow; all of his weight was behind it. It caught Pang's right jaw at an angle and he felt the snap and crunch. His jaw dropped two inches, out of control. He spun, fell sidewise against the wall, sagged, but remained on his feet.

Gates sprang at the suitcases, grabbed one, pawed through it crazily as he yelled:

"I've been waiting for this for five years. . . ."

He came up with a .45 revolver in his hands.

"Van! Van! Don't shoot!" Hazel tumbled onto the bed, scattering the bills.

Pang stared at the tunnel-like muzzle of the hand gun. He tried, but couldn't utter a sound. He seemed unable to move. He first flinched as the gun blasted its deafening thunder, then reeled, staggered, trying to hold his jaw in place with both hands. Shot after shot pounded around him. He counted, seemingly in slow motion. One. . . . two. . . . three. . . . four. . . . five. One to go!

He fell across the washbasin, blood seeping from his mouth. Boom! The last shot banged into the wall just above his head.

As though coming out of a trance, his drunken rage exhausted, Gates hurled the gun to the floor. He threw his arms around Pang, sobbing in thick-tongued contriteness:

"My God! This is the worst thing I've ever done. I'll never take a drink again."

He straightened, steadying both.

"C'mon Pang, I'll take you to the hospital. Hazel, if anybody wants to know what happened, tell 'em it's an accident."

In the emergency room the doctor found that the left side of Pang's jaw was dislocated. On the right there was a compound fracture. The physician saw the plaster which had been blown into Pang's hair when the bullets powdered the wall.

"Did you fall into a sand pit?"

"I've been shooting at him," Gates replied as though it were normal routine which had gone slightly astray.

Pang's face was put in a cast and a nurse tucked him into bed. Later he learned that one bullet had gone through the wall, wrecking the telephone in the next room. Judge, the mascot, had taken off at the first shot and had wedged himself between bathtub and wall, the first sign of apparent cowardice Judge had ever shown. Al MacLatchie, in bed in another adjoining room, had been reading a mystery thriller.

Al had just reached—"and Johnny, seeing the skulking figure wraith-like in the mist, fired twice." Bang! Bang! Gate's shots were timed exactly into Al's reading. He leaped from the bed and dived under it.

The entire circus crew came to the hospital to see Pang. His face was in a rigid pack of gauze covered with plaster of paris. His jaw hurt like hell as he listened to Ashcraft, acting as spokesman for the visitors.

"I've taken Gates's gun and he'll never have another as long as I'm around him," Big Jack said. "What do you want us to do? We'll all quit, if you want. Or we'll tell Gates he's through with this particular circus, even if he does own half."

Pang took the pad from the bedside stand. "Don't bust up the show," he wrote. "Go back to work."

As he lay in the hospital, his jaw mending, Pang had time to think, to review the status of the circus and to speculate on the future of aviation.

Charles L. Lawrence had pioneered the radial engine in the United States. He was now offering the famous 200-hp "Whirlwind" series and was testing the 450-hp "Cyclone." Pratt and Whitney Corporation, newly-formed, was rolling out the 400-hp "Wasp" with all its potential.

Planes were changing radically and growing bigger. Tony Fokker was testing his first three-engine cabin job with the hope of selling it to one of the growing American airlines. He already had a single-engine plane in service with Colonial Air Transport on its air mail route between New York and Boston. The Ford Motor Company had hired Stout and was about to mass produce the famed "tin goose." T. Claude Ryan had built his first M-1 monoplane in San Diego, and within the year would build Lindbergh's "Spirit of St. Louis" in his plant there on the former Dutch Flats where Pangborn had barnstormed in '20.

New, small, three-place open jobs were also being produced. Among them were the "Waco" of Advance Aircraft, Alexander's "Eaglerock," the Travel Air, and the innovations of Cessna and Swallow in Wichita.

Pang could see no way the circus could use these light planes equipped with war-surplus engines, which meant they were underpowered. They cost more than the circus could pay. They were delicate compared to the war-built, beefed-up Standards; they carried only two passengers while the circus must carry four to stay in the black.

While Pang recovered in the hospital, pondering the future, and luxuriated in the extra attention of the young nurses who were thrilled by their close contact with a "real" aviator, Daws conceived the zanniest stunt yet. He not only conceived it, he sold the notorious New York tabloid, the *Evening Graphic,* on promoting the stunt. The idea was to put on a wing-walking show over the Battery, up Broadway, around Times Square and over Central Park.

Daws convinced the innovative editor, Emile Gauvreau, that the stunt would show the city and the nation how really unprepared America was against air attack. Since this was a premise being propounded by General Billy Mitchell, to the dismay of his superior, General Foulois, Gauvreau saw the tie-in. At that very time Mitchell was being court-martialed for violating the 96th Article of War. He had criticized his superiors for not creating a separate Air Service.

Pangborn was discharged from the hospital, his jaw still in a cast, in time to go to New York City and watch the boys put on their show. The *Graphic* had assigned one of its top reporters, Ed Churchill, to work with Daws. He produced exciting advance stories which made residents of the five buroughs well aware of the upcoming show.

It was a gray December day when the planes took off from the Teterboro field for Manhattan. Ashcraft, Lund and Art Caperton, who had been hired to fly Pang's ship, were at the controls. Caperton, the conservative, had refused to fly until he was given a parachute.

Krantz and Wild Bill Wunderlick strutted between and on top of the wings, hung by their knees from undercarriages; did the "break-away" stunt, in which it appeared they had fallen.

The show started at the Battery in view of the Texaco Company's main office, which was fitting since Texaco was furnishing all the fuel for the circus. Then in tandem up Broadway the planes looped, whip-stalled, rolled and skidded. At times they flew below the tops of the buildings, the staccato exhaust of their engines assailing the ear-drums of the awed spectators below.

Traffic stopped. Times Square stood still, as the five zanies above were supposed to somehow be proving that the nation indeed did not have an aerial defense.

The craziness moved north, hesitated over Columbus Circle, swooped down between the trees of Central Park and then flew sedately back to the field. Pang watched from the island in Times Square, not even able to cheer.

General Mitchell was found guilty and sentenced to five years suspension of rank, pay and command. He had, however, brought military aviation to the attention of the nation. It is not likely that the cavorting over Broadway contributed significantly to the general's objective.

When his jaws were unwired so that he could talk, Pang had a long discussion with Hazel about Van.

"Why did he do it?" he asked her.

"He's been afraid of you ever since you went after him with a hammer for taking the gasoline from the drum in Salt Lake City," she said. "He knows you have no respect for him and that you have no use for drunks."

"Is that all?"

"I think he envies your abilities, the way you get along with people, your acceptance by the crew, and he knows you want no part of him socially. That's hurt him, too."

"Hell, all I ever try to do is to keep him straightened out, for his sake as well as yours—and mine."

"Don't think I don't realize that, Pang. We both want to help Van all we can. In spite of everything, I love him. Oh, God, how I love him."

Pang put his hand on her shoulder.

"I know. You can count on me."

"Thanks. I have a feeling that I'm going to need you as long as Van lives."

19

Ponce de Leon Revisits

THE WILD RUSH of the "Sooners" when Oklahoma territory was opened for settlement was nothing compared to the mad Florida land boom of the mid-'20s. So-called lots, under three feet of slimy, alligator-infested waters, were sold for fifty dollars a front foot, and resold the next day for one hundred, then sold again.

From north and west people rushed to the peninsula, attached like an appendix to the nether reaches of the land. People bought not to keep, but to resell as quickly as possible. In the confusion speculators tried to sell to each other. Promotional gimmicks approached the bizarre. Special trains carried eager buyers from all parts of the nation. Anyone indicating the least interest in buying property could criss-cross the state in one free bus after another, with complimentary meals thrown in. A special promotion brought the National Editorial Association, representatives of newspapers from throughout the country, to see the wonders of this newly discovered Eden. As anticipated these editors, would, on their return, write of the marvels they had seen.

An earlier visitor, Ponce de Leon, who likewise had been attracted by the alleged marvels of the region, was seen again. He wore winter underwear dyed purple. On his head was a wide-brimmed black hat with a long ostrich-feather plume. A scabbard was fixed to a heavy black leather belt. He held aloft a sword borrowed from a local Knight Templar and he stood, proud against the wind, on the top wing of Pangborn's Standard as they called attention to a new sub-division at De Leon Springs by circling and dipping above the over-priced ground. The pseudo Ponce was George Babcock, a wing-walker with the circus.

Like the original Ponce, Babcock failed to find the fabled fountain of youth. He was killed the following summer while making an auto-to-plane change for another circus in Minnesota.

Attracted by reports of the record crowds taxing the facilities of the Florida cities, Gates and Pangborn had taken the circus south. The crew included Jack Ashcraft, Wilmer Stultz and Eddie Bond as pilots, in addition to Pangborn. Others of the menage were Duke Krantz, Wild Bill Wunderlick, Mickey Efferson, and George Babcock, with their varied abilities as wing-walkers and parachute-jumpers. Gates, with Daws assisting, handled advance billings. Hazel and Eddie Bond's wife traveled in the Lincoln. Then there was Al MacLatchie with his kitchen tent, and a couple of roustabouts.

Stultz was new with the circus, taking the place of Eddie Brooks who had returned to California and his beloved Nelle. Stultz had a reputation for high jinx second only to that of Bert Acosta. For some reason Stultz had been irritated by the performance of Captain Charles Nungesser, the French ace, during his American tour. Stultz had jumped into his plane and flown off to engage the startled Frenchman in a violent dog fight. Asked why he had done it, Stultz replied.

"I had to show that joker Americans can fly, too."

At this peak of the land boom, Florida seemingly had more money than oranges. Gates and Daws found themselves in a world of subdividers who would pay handsomely for any stunt calling attention to their developments. Five hundred dollars for a single stunt such as a change from a boat to an airplane or a dive into the water by a wing-walker. Five or six thousand dollars for a week's show.

In addition to the exhibitions for newspapers, chambers of commerce, municipalities and land developers, a new gold mine was discovered in aerial photography. Owners who didn't know what their property looked like—the tropical growth frequently prevented ground level observation—paid well for pictures taken from the air.

Original plans to go on to Miami were abandoned. Instead the circus stayed in the wildly developing area bounded by Jacksonville and Tallahassee on the north and Daytona Beach, Sebring, St.

Petersburg and Tampa on the south. There was practically no competition. George Haldeman, who had organized a flying circus out of Lakeland just after World War I, was in the real estate business. He didn't even own a plane. His return to flying and the setting of long-distance records was to come later. Basil Rowe was operating in another part of the state, carrying passengers in a flying boat.

Eddie Bond and Pang were set to take off for a two-plane night fireworks display at Daytona Beach. The city was paying $6,000 for a week of day and night shows.

Big Jack Ashcraft offered to crank Bond's ship.

"Switch off!" Jack shouted.

"Switch off!" Bond signaled in return.

Ashcraft spun the propeller to pull a charge of gasoline into the cylinders. But it was dark in the cockpit. The switch was not off! The engine back-fired, the propeller flailed and Jack went down, his arm broken.

Mrs. Bond, who was watching, was shocked; became hysterical.

"This whole thing is too dangerous," she cried. "I won't let Eddie fly the fireworks. He'll be killed."

Eddie jumped from the cockpit and, with Hazel, tried to calm his wife.

"Get Bill Stultz to fly it," Mrs. Bond mumbled.

"Bill's in town," Pang told her.

"Jack could have flown it," the distraught woman continued. "Jack's single. If he gets killed, he won't ruin a wife's life. . . ."

Pang chalked up one more reason for not hiring a married pilot, as Jack sighed:

"Oh, hell, I'll fly it."

Over Pangborn's protests Big Jack pulled himself into the plane and yelled:

"Eddie, crank me up!"

"Jack, you can't. . . ."

"The hell I can't. The contract calls for two planes in the air. If there aren't, we don't get paid. Let's go!"

The two planes took off, put on their spectacular fireworks show, fulfilled the contract. Then Pang took Jack to a doctor to have the arm set.

Money rolled in as the tremendous business continued. The pilots—Ashcraft, Stultz and Bond—were making more than three thousand dollars a month. They received 15 or 20 per cent of the revenue from the passengers they carried and they shared in the booming paid exhibitions. Their percentage of the gross on special shows at Daytona Beach and Davis Island netted each $1,100. With his usual indifference, Pangborn was drawing enough for his living requirements and the modest amounts he spent on clothes and entertainment. The remainder of his share of the profits he left to accumulate in the hands of the Gateses, assuring himself he could draw it whenever he might want to.

Despite the promises of eternal sunshine in the Florida promotion material, an occasional storm would come in from its breeding place in the Caribbean. In the face of one such threatening blow, Pang ordered extra tie-towns for all the planes. Stultz didn't do a good job, so the next morning his plane was a jumble of kindling, having been blown across the field like a tumbleweed.

"I'm gonna get drunk," he announced.

The drunk lasted for a week while the circus traveled from St. Petersburg to Daytona. He sometimes disappeared for hours. At Daytona Pang fired him. Stultz accepted it matter-of-fact, took the $3,000 due him and headed north. His next job was as pilot for Charles Levine, the Brooklyn junk dealer whom Clarence D. Chamberlin flew to Germany, and Mabel Boll, "The Queen of Diamonds," a character who was flashing her way through the glistening twenties.

With spring the great Florida land boom started to dwindle, and with the budding trees and greening fields beckoning, the circus headed north. It now had six five-place Standards, with 180-horsepower, high-compression Hispano-Suiza engines. New members of the crew were Buck Steele, Joseph H. James, Wallace Goldberry, Jack Parks, Charles (Slim) West and John Miller. The latter two were mechanics, the others, pilots, wing-walkers or parachute-jumpers.

A tight, smooth and efficient organization had been effected. Henry (Happy) Johnson had been sent to Germantown to set up an engine overhaul base. Now a telegram to Happy brought a newly overhauled Hisso by express. Daws, working as advance man, had a new Dodge touring car. He was accompanied by a billposter who distributed broadsides in shop windows, on fences and the sides of buildings, any place where they would attract attention.

The circus continued to work with newspapers, chambers of commerce, fraternal organizations and civic bodies. Newspapermen were taken for rides over their cities, newspapers delivered to outlying points, and toy parachutes carrying prizes and tickets for rides were dropped. The personnel numbered more than 20 and the circus was grossing more than two-hundred thousand dollars a year.

It was the big cities now, as well as the cow-pasture towns; Atlanta, Birmingham, Albany, Chattanooga, Cincinnati, Cleveland, Daytona, Louisville, Pittsburgh, Troy, Wheeling. From these major points the circus covered the surrounding smaller communities capitalizing on publicity generated in the area.

On the way north out of Jacksonville Pang dropped in on St. Simon's Island for a visit with Howard Coffin, aviation enthusiast, who was the principal backer of Paul Redfern. Redfern had taken off from Brunswick, Georgia on a flight to Rio de Janeiro, and in one of aviation's greatest mysteries, disappeared completely.

For years rumors of Redfern persisted. He was the white chief of a tribe in the Amazon jungle; he was in perfect health after crashing; he was badly crippled; he had set up a small kingdom in the jungle and was extremely wealthy. Numerous expeditions were proposed; their objective to find Redfern. Pang had been asked to head two of these, in one of which Errol Flynn was involved. Pang regarded all the proposals as mere publicity stunts. In his view the fate of Redfern was simple; he had been lost at sea or had crashed fatally in dense jungle.

At Decatur, Georgia, Gates and Pangborn earned an easy $250. The Stone Mountain Memorial Committee had just fired Gutzon Borglum from the job of carving a Confederate bas-relief on the side of Stone Mountain. General Lee was only partially finished. The committee asked Gates and Pangborn if they could make an aerial photograph of the work that had been completed by Borglum.

"We want a close-up," the committee specified, "with lots of detail."

"Suppose we shoot it at about twenty-five feet?" Pangborn asked. The committee members chuckled at the joke.

With Gates and his camera in the rear cockpit, Pang made two passes along the face of the mountain, checking for jutting rocks.

Then, on the third pass, he went in close with his wingtip only a few feet from the solid rock. The committee was delighted with the pictures; they were exactly what was wanted.

Pang had a feeling however that things were going too smoothly. In Chattanooga he got a call as he was dressing in his hotel room. It was from Gates and he obviously was highly agitated.

"Get the hell down to the lobby!" he boomed.

In the lobby Pang found his partner striding up and down, waving a newspaper, anger flashing from those squint eyes.

"What's eating you?"

"Did you see this goddam newspaper?" Gates stormed. "Coolidge has signed that damned Bingham-Parker Act. We're going to have a goddamn bunch of bureaucrats telling us how to fly our planes, when we can go to the john. . .

"Pang, those bastards in the government are going to bar night fireworks, any kind of plane change. We're going to have inspectors going over our planes; got to have 'em licensed. No more stunting over business districts. Gotta fly hundreds of feet apart. Gotta fly so high and so far from the fields the suckers can't see what we're doing. Hell, we're through!"

Gates ripped the newspaper, threw it to the floor, then stomped on it.

"Van, you're blowing a gasket. Some day you'll wind up in a coffin if you don't stop losing your temper. Look, those regulations won't become effective for months. You know the government, it'll take them years to get things set up. We can just keep going as we are until they tell us to lay off."

"Goddamn it, Pang, they're taking the bread out of our mouths. they're. . . ."

"Let's have breakfast," Pang said as Gates' anger slowly cooled.

To himself, Pang had to admit that things were getting tougher. They were clashing more and more with local, fixed-base operators who didn't want competition in their territory. The lines having mail contracts were also beginning to carry passengers. The Post Office Department was letting new contracts each month. U.S. manufacturers had produced 789 airplanes during the year. This meant more competition for the circus. No doubt the new Air Commerce Act and Air Commerce Regulations would severely restrict stunt flying.

For some time Pang had pondered that perhaps the crazy stunts they were performing were scaring away potential passengers. Did people want to fly with pilots who performed this way? He was worried about acrobatics. He felt that more people came to the fields against the possibility of seeing a crash or a wing-walker fall, than to take to the air themselves. Possibly a conservative stunting program to demonstrate the sturdiness of the aircraft would attract rather than repel passengers.

Was a new day, a new approach ahead for the circus, or was the new competition—the regulations and restrictions—a portent that would write "finis" to barnstorming?

20

Uncle Sam Steps In

"PANG, WE NEED a spot where we can overhaul before we go south again," Gates declared. "I think maybe I can make a deal for Teterboro Airport, over there below Hasbrouck Heights, New Jersey."

"Clarence Chamberlin's old field," Pang replied. "Fokker's in there now. Sounds like a good idea. All the ships need plenty of fixing."

"The way we're growing, I think we need a permanent base. I'm scared of these air regulations; they'll lick barnstorming. We gotta have an ace up our sleeve. Maybe a flying school, or fixed base work, charter flights, photography—even build our own airplanes. Who knows?"

Gates leased full operational rights at Teterboro. Then in nearby Lodi he found an abandoned rubber factory and rented it as an overhaul base. Finally he booked the entire crew into a medium priced hotel on Broadway.

That evening, the bright red supply truck, with its modest sign, "The World's Greatest Aviators," rolled to a stop in front of the hotel. Gaping pedestrians gathered, as they do on New York streets at the slightest deviation from the usual. A dozen booted, mustached, helmeted characters poured from the rear of the truck where they had sat amid gasoline containers, spare wheels, tires and coils of rope.

New York crowds proved too much, and the distance from Teterboro too far, so the crew moved into the Alexander Hotel in Paterson, N.J.

At midnight, January 1, 1927, the Department of Commerce Air Regulations of the Air Commerce Act went into effect. The domestic airlines of the nation had carried 5,782 passengers during the year. The scruffy, patched and weather-beaten planes of the Gates Flying Circus, with a doubtful value of only a few thousand dollars, had carried more than 200,000 passengers, flying from the improvised fields of a hundred cities in a score of states.

For Pangborn, highlight of the year had been his creation of a plane of unique design and distinct appearance. It was composed of four Aeromarine lower wings, a few Standard parts and a four-passenger cockpit which featured a flexible hood giving it a semi-closed cabin effect. The top of the cockpit had a top with a spring attachment. As the passengers loaded it was in an upright position. Then when the Hispano-Suiza engine came to life, the propeller blast would blow the top down to a closed position. After landing, and the engine had been shut down, the spring would raise the top again, like a gentleman tipping his hat to a lady.

The extra wide undercarriage and the bulging cabin top made the craft, when viewed from the front, look like a man sitting on a low seat in a Chick Sales.

Gates had arranged a significant dinner. It was given in honor of the Aeronautics Branch of The Department of Commerce and particularly for Parker D. (Shorty) Cramer, the former barnstormer, now an inspector of the newly formed governmental bureau.

The enforcement group of the Department was not much larger than the Gates Circus. Clarence M. Young was chief of air regulations; Louis H. Bauer, the medical director. Then there were Ralph G. Lockwood, supervising inspector; John L. Hosch, aeronautical engineer; five inspectors of aircraft and engines, and Frank H. Jerdone, experimental pilot.

"We wish to do the right thing," Gates told the guests. "If you and the government tell us we must meet certain requirements for licensing our airplanes we intend to meet those requirements. We expect you, Mr. Cramer, to tell us exactly what you want and we will do those things.

"Perhaps we have been a bit remiss. Perhaps we have let our equipment deteriorate. It is only fair that we should have regulatory action and so I call on you, sir."

Cramer arose to his full five feet five inches.

"Your airplanes do not meet the new requirements. Your flying circus is through!"

Gates snorted, his eyes reduced to peepholes.

"This is the goddamndest thing I've ever heard in my life. You, Cramer, think you can kill our living. Well, you're wrong, I'm going to Washington to prove it. You've overlooked one thing. Our airplanes can fly!"

Gates returned from Washington, elated in victory. He had determined that the new regulations were not formed to put the circus out of business. Cramer was ordered to remain with the circus until the airplanes had been modified and could be licensed. Up to that time the circus had carried nearly a half-million passengers with only one fatality. Certainly the planes could fly; but now they must also be flyable technically.

The bright red planes were powered with the V-8 Hisso engines; good engines, but heavy in relation to horsepower developed. They were water-cooled, which added weight. They were hard to start on cold mornings. If the valves needed grinding, it was done on the spot. If something more serious had developed, a wire to Happy Johnson for a rebuilt would get immediate response.

The airframes had been in very poor condition. Wing by wing, fuselage by fuselage, they were taken to the Lodi facility. There they had been stripped, recovered, doped and painted. Split beams were spliced, damaged ribs replaced. Wires were tightened, metal parts renewed. And as the work was completed, Cramer granted the licenses which were needed if the circus was to continue flying.

The crew was shocked later when Cramer and Oliver Pacquette were lost at sea during an attempted transatlantic flight from Detroit to Denmark.

Pilots, too, had to be licensed. With several thousand hours in his log book Pang was able to convince Daniel deR. M. Scarrett, one of the department inspectors, that he could indeed get an airplane off the ground and back in one piece. He was issued license number 240.

Perhaps inspired by the licensing requirement for the pilots, Gates decided to learn to fly, after all the years during which he had recounted tales of his aerial abilities. Buck Steele had already permitted him to take the controls in the air on a few occasions. Now he found an elderly and very cautious pilot who gave him eight hours of intense instruction.

At the end of that time, and reviewing Gates's capabilities, the instructor turned him loose with:

"Now, you son-of-a-bitch, go ahead and kill yourself."

To celebrate his solo and the conquering of his mortal fear of airplanes, Gates took Hazel to Cuba for a three weeks binge.

Pangborn was delighted to have Gates out of his hair. The circus always seemed to operate more smoothly when Gates wasn't around to interfere and cause confusion. Pang was also amazed as the money accumulated in amounts he had not been aware of.

21

The Circus Reaches Its Peak

GATHERED AROUND a static-squealing radio in Vincennes, Indiana, the circus crew learned that Lindbergh had landed safely at LeBourget on the outskirts of Paris. His flight put the exclamation point behind what Pangborn and the circus had been trying to demonstrate—that flying was safe, that a new era of transportation needed only to be developed.

Pangborn felt that there were scores of pilots who were capable of having made the flight. He, himself, had approached Will Dodge of the Texas Company seeking backing for a trans-Atlantic flight. He conceded, however, that Lindbergh had the guts and the skill to accomplish the feat, and had proved it through a day and a night in a small airplane through abominable weather.

Lindbergh's flight accomplished what the circus had not been able to do in eight years of trying to awaken the general public to aviation. The flight boosted aircraft manufacturing, gave impetus to air transportation, gave the circus a new lease on life and engendered a series of long distance flights, some successful, some tragic.

Even as Lindbergh set off on a nation-wide tour in "The Spirit of St. Louis," Stout began passenger service between Detroit and Cleveland; American Railway Express started operations; Maddox Airlines started on the west coast and new air mail contracts were being issued in Washington.

Aircraft production more than doubled from 1,995 planes in

1927 to 4,761 in 1928. Among prominent manufacturers in the industry were Boeing, Bellanca, Consolidated, Douglas, Fairchild, Glen L. Martin, Sikorsky, Stinson, and Travel Air.

After excitement of the ocean flight had subsided, the circus settled into its normal routine. A sweep through Michigan, Indiana and Illinois took them into Ohio. Increasingly they were encountering opposition from local operators who felt the circus was taking business from them. At Warren, Ohio, the local operator complained to the Department of Commerce inspector that the circus airplanes were in "terrible condition."

In other communities supplies were stolen from the truck, mud and sugar were put in gasoline tanks, advertising posters and arrows showing direction to the fields were torn down. Violations of local ordinances were frequently charged. In one instance an operator argued that Indian land was for agricultural use and could not be leased out by the Indians as a landing field.

In Pennsylvania "Whispering Bill" Brooks rejoined the circus, accompanied by "Major" Lee Mason. Mason had the unique ability to smoke a pipe while flying in an open cockpit. He was the envy of the other fliers.

Brooks brought a fantastic tale of the duo's exploits during a stint in Central America. With gusto he related:

"Can't tell you how we done it, but we're in with the nationals down there in Nicaragua. We flew out of Managua, chasin' this here General Augustino Sandino and his rebels.

"It's a swell deal. We get paid in gold—solid gold. We fly these here OX 5 Swallows. We don't have any machine guns, but this ain't no worry.

"Now, how we go after this here Sandino and his jungle boys is something. Lee and me make bombs. We make these here bombs out of gallon cans filled with dynamite, and a bunch of bolts and nuts. We put 'em in our laps and take off, me smoking a cigar, Lee smoking his pipe.

"Well, we get out over the jungle where we figure these Sandino boys are hidin', light the fuses with our smokes. Then we heave-ho. Brother, what a bang we make!

"I don't think we kill any, but the noise makes them scatter. Then we land. It's that easy."

The crew lines up with five Standards at Williamsport, Pennsylvania, in 1927. Left to right: Charles (Slim) West, Jack Ashcraft, (unknown), Duke Krantz, Pangborn, Van Gates, (unknown), Samuel (Buck) Steele, (unknown), Mickey Efferson, Al McClatchie, (unknown), George Daws, Eddie Brooks, (unknown), and Shorty Bittner.

"Suppose you came home because you ran out of bolts and nuts," Gates said in his usual sarcastic manner.

"Hell, no! The goddamn U. S. Marines landed."

At Johnston, Pennsylvania, a youth, not very tall, appeared at the field, carrying a dilapidated satchel.

"I'm Shorty Bittner," he said. "I want a job with this outfit. I've got a lot of experience—seventeen hours."

"How'd you get to the field," Pangborn asked.

"Walked."

"How far is it?"

"Fifteen miles."

"Well, Bittner, if you want a job with us that badly, you're hired. But only as a mechanic."

Bittner was given to practical jokes. He nearly drove Pangborn crazy on one occasion by getting under his plane and tapping with a hammer in cadence with the engine. The gang looked on with glee while Pang spent an anxious five minutes searching before he discovered the source of the "knock."

At Terre Haute a new $110 propeller had been put on Buck Steel's plane. Bittner and some others were to tow it across the field. Shorty rigged a stout towing wire from the truck axle to the plane's spreader bar on the landing gear. Then he tied an old rope onto the new propeller, climbed into the truck and pretended that the rope was doing the towing. Gates raced across the field, ready to take Bittner apart, when he discovered the hoax. Shorty shriveled under Gates' blast.

Now a six-plane operation, the circus moved on into New Jersey. George Bruce, the advance man, had booked flying privileges on a large estate. Landing there Pang left a teenager to watch the plane while he went into town for lunch. When he returned he found two young girls having fun on the ship.

"Get off there," he snapped.

A local whispered in his ear: "You better be careful. One of those girls is Doris Duke."

"Who's she?"

"She just owns this place, that's all. She's one of the richest girls in the world."

Then about 14, Doris hadn't seemed to mind being shouted at. Smiling and pretty, she waved at Pang each time he took off with passengers, which happened about 25 times that particular afternoon.

The three-day extravaganza was advertised as "The National Air Show." It represented the peak achievement of the Gates Flying Circus' 10-year history. There were eleven planes, all in the circus colors, on the line.

"Count 'em, ladies and gentlemen," Leo (Red) Murphy spieled from the tail of the truck. "And each and every one is licensed; piloted by the finest collection of aviators in the world. Yes sir, the greatest fliers in the world."

An eager crowd had been attracted by the publicity campaign put on by George Daws, George Bruce and Ed Churchill. The latter had been hired on a temporary basis from the *New York Graphic*.

The pilots lined up with boots shined, trousers pressed to razor sharpness, helmets and goggles under their arms. They included Roy Ahearn, who had had 26 forced landings bringing a Standard L6 from Chicago, Ive McKinney, "Whispering Bill" Brooks, Jack Ashcraft, Okey Bevins, little Buck Steele, Major Lee Mason, Harold McMahon, Warren B. Smith, and, of course, Pangborn.

Gates was in his glory as he savored his title of "Director-General." He wore boots, breeches and a white shirt. The outfit was topped with a decidedly incongruous straw hat.

The crowd surged and broke through the ropes which had been set up to restrain them. Gates' short fuse had burned its length.

"Get those people back, goddamn it!" he bellowed. "Get them back!"

No one moved to action. "I'm going crazy," he ranted, slamming his straw hat on the ground and smashing it with several jumps. "I'm going crazy."

One of the crew pushed the overflowing crowd back behind the rope. Solemnly he said:

"Have some respect, folks. Stand back. Can't you see that a man's going crazy here?"

As a special feature of the show Pangborn demonstrated his invention—air mail pick-up.

The circus reaches its peak. Eleven airplanes including Jennies, Standards, a Bellanca, and a Curtiss R. The planes were lined up at the National Airplane Show at Teterboro in 1927.

Two poles with hooks on the upper ends were held by two men about 20 feet apart. A rope ran between the hooks, the ends carried down and backward where they were fastened to a simulated mail bag. Pang flew by with a hook under his plane, snared the rope, and pulled the bag into the cockpit.

When the "national" show prepared to go on the road, Gates said to Pangborn, very mysteriously: "Pretty soon I'll have some news that will set you on your ear."

He did indeed have a surprise: the Gates-Day Aircraft Corporation of Paterson, New Jersey. It was to manufacture an entirely new airplane. According to Gates, every operator would want to buy one. The company would flood the nation with open-cockpit barnstorming planes.

Gates had brought in Charles Healy Day who had been designing and building airplanes since shortly after the Wright brothers and Glen Curtiss first flew. He was the designer and builder of the Standards which the circus had been operating for several years.

The assets and name of the Gates Flying Circus were fixed at $50,000. Day's plans and drawings for his GD-24 were valued at $10,000. The "G" stood for Gates, the "D" for Day. Gates talked himself into the presidency of the corporation, Day became vice-president, Pangborn, a director, assistant to the chief engineer and chief test pilot. The circus was made a subsidiary of the corporation with Pangborn as president.

The circus took to the road, buoyed by a coup engineered by Daws. He had made a tie-up with Thomas Hill, of the American Society for the Promotion of Aviation. The circus was to operate under auspices of the society and would carry passengers at $1.00 each to increase interest in flying. It made the circus a non-profit, benevolent, charitable organization. Newspapers and various organizations would naturally be interested in helping promote an organization dedicated to educating the American public.

Free from Gates' interference and the drain of his "entertainment and expenses," the circus was making money faster than Pangborn thought was possible. After a single day's flying, Pang threw more than $3,000 in small bills onto his bed and drew the spread over the take as he went to eat. Frantic messages and telephone calls were coming in from Gates asking for money to keep the manufacturing enterprise going. Due to the circus's success Pang was able to send an amazing amount of money to the Paterson operation.

Bone weary, the crew took the circus back to Teterboro for overhaul of aircraft and engines. For the first time, under the new corporate set-up, Pang had made substantial money. He collected on the basis of 20 per cent of the receipts. He had made only a bare living while receiving 50 per cent under the Gates-Pangborn partnership.

When he arrived in Paterson he had a suitcase full of bills of all denominations. Most of the bills were wrapped in newspapers, held together with rubber bands. The suitcase had been shoved under the bed and remained there for several weeks. One day while a friend was visiting, Pang pulled out the suitcase and opened it.

"What the hell are all those bundles?" the friend asked.

"Money."

"What kind of money?"

"Bills."

"How much?"

"About twenty-five grand I guess."

The friend clapped his hands to his head. "Good God in heaven. Get that dough to the bank!"

Pang finally agreed to bank the money in Lodi. He walked into the bank alone, carrying the suitcase.

"I'd like to make a deposit," he said to a teller at one of the windows.

"That's fine," the teller replied. "Where is your money?"

Pang replied that it was quite a bit and he had it in the suitcase he was carrying. The teller suggested that Pang go around behind his cage to a desk and count it.

As Pang opened the case several bundles fell to the floor and broke open. All hell broke loose. Doors banged, bells rang, a siren sounded. Then the police came, shotguns at the ready.

"Where did you get this money," a bank official demanded, his bravado augmented by the policeman at each elbow.

"Running a flying circus."

Neither the bank officials nor the police would believe the story. Pang referred them to the Gates-Day Corporation and to several prominent citizens of the area whom he knew. Finally a number of telephone calls convinced them that Pang had not robbed a bank and that the money was his.

He watched with satisfaction as the tellers spent most of the afternoon counting the small bills.

While the equipment was being overhauled, Gates and Pangborn talked of buying a big cabin monoplane.

"People want to ride in these new jobs," Pangborn said. "It would be a real attraction for the circus, and carrying a lot of passengers at one time should pay off the investment in a short time."

"Sounds good," Gates agreed. "Let's go see Tony Fokker. He's built an F-14A, a single-engine cabin job that'll carry fourteen passengers. I think it's just what we want."

Always dealing on a cash basis, Gates habitually carried large sums of money. At the moment he had some $30,000 in large denomination bills in his wallet.

The two went to the Fokker factory. Fokker, Robert Noorduyn, his sales manager, and other officers of the company were sunning themselves outside the office. Gates pointed to the F-14 nearby, glistening in its newness.

"How much for that?" he asked the famous designer.

"Just $28,000," Fokker replied. He added in sarcasm, "that is, if you had $28,000, of course."

Gates blew another fuse.

"Why, you Dutch son-of-a-bitch, after that crack I wouldn't buy a rusty bolt from you!"

Taking out his wallet, he waved the $30,000 under the startled and disappointed nose of the designer.

Gates and Pang left. Pang declared later that it was a major mistake not to have bought a large, modern aircraft. While they might have missed a sale, the Fokker boys were sharpies.

Ray Howard, test pilot, who was working on the Fokker Universal, asked Pang one day if he wouldn't like to fly the new plane. The next morning at the field Pang found the plane warmed up. Howard, and Raymond S. Quick, engineering test pilot for the Department of Commerce, were waiting. Quick had been assigned by the Department to run acceptance tests on this new model.

As Pang was about to enter the plane, Howard said:

"Why don't you giver her a couple of spins while you're up?"

Pang took off and found that the plane flew perfectly. Then he wrung it out . . . loops, slow rolls, and a couple of spins. When he landed, the Fokker men, including Tony, Noorduyn, Hughie Wells, and several others gaped, mouths open. They all talked at once, plying questions about the plane's spinning qualities.

"What's all this about spins?" Pang asked.

Wells spoke up: "That's the first time she's been spun."

Pang learned that he had been taken. Howard and the others wouldn't spin the new job. Yet Quick, the department test pilot, couldn't run his official tests until spins had been completed. Pang had done the job for free!

The Fokker Universal proved to be an excellent airplane. One of the first to take delivery was Eddie Brooks, who was flying for Albert E. Humphries of the Humphries Oil Company of Denver.

22

The Ranks Thin

ANOTHER FUNERAL; another flying friend and associate "gone west." It seemed to Pang that the sad occasions had become more frequent. He pondered that while the circus had flown nearly a half million passengers, with only one fatal accident and had never lost a pilot, death among the former pilots and performers of the circus had seemingly become epidemic.

Had he not been busy testing the New Standards, this latest rite might well have been for him; instead it was for friendly, eager Jack Ashcraft. Endurance flights were the craze of the day. The Army airplane "The Question Mark," commanded by Major "Tooey" Spaatz, with Captain Ira Eaker as co-pilot, had stayed in the air for 150 hours.

Viola Gentry, a restaurant hostess, seeking fame, had acquired an airplane she dubbed "The Answer." She had come to Pangborn and asked him to fly her in an attempt to beat "The Question Mark" record.

"I'm too busy," he told her. "But I know a good man."

"Who?"

"Jack Ashcraft," Pang replied, knowing that Jack, over at Holmes airport, was available.

So Jack and Viola had taken off in their Paramount Cabinaire. They were to be refueled in the air by Carl Dixon. On the fourth scheduled refueling, heavy fog over Connecticut prevented Dixon from taking off. With his fuel exhausted, Ashcraft had to come down for a blind crash landing. The plane sheared off a tree. Jack was killed. Viola was horribly injured, but eventually recovered.

There had been a rumor that Jack, of short snorter fame, had taken a bottle aloft with him, though it had no bearing on the fact that the refueling plane couldn't get off the ground, nor that Jack had to make a blind landing in the fog.

Bill Stultz, who with Lou Gordon had flown Amelia Earhart across the Atlantic before she did it on her own, came to Pangborn after the services for Jack.

"This is hell," Stultz said. "I hear old Jack took a supply of liquor with him. That's taught me a lesson. I'll never take another drink!"

A short time later Stultz went up with a couple of bootleggers at Roosevelt Field. A passenger jammed his foot between the end of the rudder bar and the fuselage as Bill was stunting. The sheared foot and a shoe was found there in the fatal crash wreckage.

Wally Goldberry, who had worked with the circus in Ohio and Pennsylvania, later spun in at Chillicothe, Ohio, when a student froze on the controls. It was reported that a farmer, stripping fabric from the wreck, looked it over and hurled it aside commenting: "No blood."

While on tour with the Flying Fleet, Pangborn had scattered flowers over the burial place of Phil Leiniger in Pueblo, Colorado and that of Ive McKinney, near Medford, Oregon.

The death of McKinney was typically ironic. His first brush with disaster was when he flew a homemade plane at Teterboro. The two youths who had built it asked McKinney to test fly it. He ended with the engine in his lap and a stay of several weeks in the hospital. After recovering he went to Wilmington, Delaware and asked Guiseppi Bellanca for a job as test pilot.

"Sure you can have a job," Bellanca replied. "Hop into that plane over there and give it a try."

But Ive was superstitious. He remembered that it was Friday the thirteenth. No flying against that omen of trouble. As he drove away from the field a heavily loaded coal truck turned over on his car and fractured his skull. Back to the hospital.

"The busted head isn't so bad, but I can't stand those goddamn nurses arguing over me," he said.

Crash of "The Answer" in which Jack Ashcraft was killed and Viola Gentry seriously injured. They were attempting to break the record set by the Army's "The Question Mark."

Some weeks later he crashed a Swallow trainer during a race at Teterboro.

"They can't kill old Ive," he mumbled as they took him from the wreckage. He died a few hours later.

The woman of his current affections went to the Teterboro officials. She asked that all the planes be cleared from the largest hangar on the field for the coming Satruday night. She put on a rip-snorting dance. The proceeds went for McKinney's funeral.

Freddie Lund, after he left the circus, became one of the nation's finest stunt fliers. His speciality was the outside loop. Jimmy Doolittle was said to have been the first to do the spectacular loop in a military plane.

Lund was killed during a race at Lexington, Kentucky, when he collided with another plane as he was rounding a pylon during a race.

Roy Ahearn made money operating the one-plane Red Wing Flying Circus after he left Gates and Pangborn. He, "Whispering Bill" Brooks, Raymond S. Quick and Carl Vickery all were killed in crashes of various kinds.

Even Happy Johnson, the skilled mechanic, lost his life. He had flown far out into the Atlantic with Marion Gravenburg in a Sikorsky S-37 equipped with pontoons to pick up pictures of the assassination of King Alexander of Yugoslavia. The Sikorsky snagged a pontoon on a wave and nosed over. Happy couldn't swim and went down before a rescue boat could reach the plane. Gravenberg was rescued.

Pangborn, who had not expected to live until he was twenty-five, had now recorded more than 10,000 hours of flying in his log book. Only four other men in the world had as many hours as Pang. They were: E. Hamilton Lee, James H. Knight, Robert Thomas and Edwin Jaquith.

Pangborn had always feared death; rather, he had deep respect for all those elements which could threaten a pilot's life. If one had that respect, was properly cautious, then fate was the master. If your number came up, it came up. Only it seemed to come up with increasing frequency in his circle of friends and associates.

23

Ashes to Ashes

GATES AND PANGBORN were attending an air show in Chicago. Pang was there to demonstrate the New Standard, Gates hoping to take orders. For two days Gates had been drunk and more obnoxious than usual. As a result his possessions had been moved out of his room in a large Chicago hotel.

Gates had stormed to the manager's office.

"You don't know who I am! I'll get your job for this!"

His fists were doubled, his eyes their usual angry slits. The hotel man sensed real trouble and pressed a buzzer which summoned two house detectives.

They didn't arrive fast enough.

Gates smashed the manager in the face.

Word of Gates' straying off the reservation reached Day and the other airplane company officials in Paterson. They wired Gates to return at once.

"Since when," he demanded, "is anybody telling me what to do?"

The Chicago affair was only the latest in a long series—going back to the National Air Races at Los Angeles. Not only was Gates' wild behavior hurting the business, he also had demonstrated very poor business judgment.

The GD-24, at his insistence, had first been listed at $1,850, later raised to $3,600. In its latest version, powered with the Wright J-5 engine, it sold for $10,750—still less than its production cost.

The situation was critical. At a tense meeting of the officers, with

Gates threatening as usual, he was offered $50,000 to get out. Faced with the unanimous opposition, Gates accepted the offer and resigned.

After being ousted by his partners in the aircraft company and blowing the $50,000 they had paid him, Gates opened a flying school and passenger service at Holmes Airport on Long Island. He also obtained the United States manufacturing rights for the Belgian RSV, renaming it the Gates-RSV trainer. It was a two-seater which could be flown either as a biplane or monoplane. The field was renamed Grand Central Airport but pilots still referred to it as "Holmes." The depression overtook both it and Gates' operations.

Ever the show man, Gates leased space in a building just off Broadway on Fifty-third Street. There he exhibited female nudes. In the summer he took the exhibition to Coney Island. When he returned to the city in the fall he found that new landlords of his former space didn't want to lease to him.

Thanksgiving eve, 1932, Gates and another pilot attended a meeting at a New York hangar of that unique organization the Quiet Birdmen. Under the slight excuse of the coming holiday, they became very drunk. When the evening session was over they stayed on alone in the clubrooms and proceeded to break up the piano and other articles of furniture.

On the mantle over the fireplace were rows of mugs each bearing the name of a member. When a member "went west" his mug was turned upside down.

Gates staggered to the mantle; turned over his own mug. Then he took a taxi to his apartment spilling change in the gutter as he fumbled to pay the driver.

At two o'clock in the morning Pangborn's telephone rang.

"Is this Pangborn," a male voice asked.

"Yes."

"Mrs. Gates wants to speak to you."

Pangborn's first reaction was that Gates had beat her up again and that she was leaving him for one of her periodic absences.

Hazel sobbed hysterically into the phone: "Pang, Van's jumped out the window of our apartment—come down quick."

When he arrived by taxi Pangborn saw a crumbled broken form on the sidewalk beneath a blanket and a uniformed officer standing beside it.

Photo courtesy of American Hall of Aviation History, Northrop University.

Early publicity poster of the Gates Flying Circus.

"You Pangborn?"

"Yes."

"Do you recognize this body," the policeman asked as he pulled back the blanket.

"Yes, it's Gates."

In the apartment, amid sobs, Hazel told Pangborn that Van had come home in an ugly mood. He had mumbled about doublecross, lousy business, no good friends. Then, he had asked for a glass of milk. After finishing it he had slammed down the glass and said:

"I'll settle everything!"

He had then rushed to the window and climbed out.

Just as he fell, Hazel grabbed a leg of his trousers. She could hold on only momentarily.

At the rites at the Campbell Mortuary, Hazel was hysterical. As she recognized Gates's former friends and associates when they came in, she would burst into a new flood of tears. Then, when Pangborn escorted her toward the casket she said: "I want to kiss him."

Pangborn tried to dissuade her, afraid that she would go to pieces completely. But she insisted, putting her lips against his cold face, and then getting complete control of herself.

Gates had many times in the past told Pangborn that he favored cremation, but Hazel wanted to bury him in California. Pangborn, with the help of Hazel's friends, persuaded her to abide by Gates' wishes. He was cremated and Pangborn, leading a three-plane formation with Clarence Chamberlin and Marion Gravenberg, scattered the ashes over Holmes Airport.

When the planes landed, Margie Doeg, who had ridden with Pang, said to the others:

"That was an amazing thing. When Van's ashes were tossed out they didn't fall—they went out and up!"

Ashes to ashes! Pangborn recalled how he and Gates had first met—in the ashes of a burned spot on a field in Yreka California.

24

—and Then They Took Away the Sky

FOLLOWING THE OUSTING of Gates, the name of the Gates-Day company was changed to "The New Standard Aircraft Corporation." The plane was redesignated the D-24. Though it had excellent performance qualities, it had one major fault. It was hopelessly out of date. It was designed for two primary purposes; to carry passengers around an airport and as an air mail transport with pilot and passengers in open cockpits exposed to the weather. A dozen manufacturers were producing cabin planes with both pilot and passengers enclosed for comfort. The adverse factors of the D-24 were obvious to any prospective buyer.

The tired circus continued to pour money into the manufacturing end of the corporation. Pangborn argued futilely that since they had to demonstrate the New Standards, the circus should be equipped with them, killing two birds with one stone. His associates disagreed and the Gates Flying Circus (the Gates name was still retained because of the publicity build-up over the years) died quietly in Florida in the late spring of 1929.

A major distributor of the New Standards was Empire Air Transport of Syracuse, headed by Garland Latta and Emil Roth, with Hugh Brewster as manager. Still convinced that barnstorming and demonstrating could be combined, Pangborn urged Roth to put a circus on the road.

As a result four New Standards flew out of Syracuse on August 3, 1929. Ed Churchill, the aviation writer from the *Graphic,* was advance man, while Bill Brooks, from the old Gates circus set-up, was one of the pilots.

The Empire Air Circus played 30 cities and was enjoying amazing success until one pilot got his low wing into the slipstream of another while making a turn after take-off at Hamilton, Ohio. Two passengers were killed in the crash. Brewster ordered the planes to return to Syracuse.

Between August 3 and November 4, the four airplanes had grossed just under $50,000. However, there was no net. A $10,000 plane was lost in the crash, another pilot had taxied into a plane while his attention was distracted, another had smashed a landing gear, and for some unfathomable reason, Brooks had spent $1,000 for a steam caliope!

Business at Canton was less than half the normal for a city of that size, a foreboding of what was to come. The date there followed immediately the first serious drop in the stock market. Full significance of the impact was slow in coming.

Even in the face of tour results, Brooks demanded that Churchill

John W. Underwood photo collection.

New Standard D-24.

go to the Franklin automobile factory in Syracuse and get him a new model for free.

"Why?" Churchill asked.

"Well, they gave one to Lindbergh, didn't they?"

After seeing the Empire Circus start on its brief career, Pangborn took three of the New Standards west on a demonstration tour. Pilots of the other two planes were Carl Dixon, ex-RFC, and Hugh Herndon, Jr., scion of a wealthy family, who was just learning to fly. Herndon had bought a Standard, cracked it up at Princeton, New Jersey, purchased another and asked to go along on the western trip. Happy Johnson, the ace mechanic, completed the crew.

At Amarillo, Pangborn ran into Lowell Yerex. He had a fantastic tale to tell of his experiences after he, Lil, and Ace, the police dog, had left the Gates outfit. The first years were prosaic; he had run a garage for several years and had taught school for a year. Moving back toward flying he became the manager of a small airline which was operating between Fort Worth and Amarillo. The crash of a new cabin monoplane, killing all on board, marked the end of the little airline.

Yerex, without a job, drifted through Mexico and on to Honduras, where he became involved in one of the innumerable revolutions characteristic of the Central American countries. Fortunately he had chosen the side which was eventually to take over the government. While flying for them he was shot in the forehead, the bullet destroying the sight of his left eye. He went to New Orleans, had the eye removed and a glass one substituted.

"After the revolution was over and the party I had signed up with had won," Yerex related, "I started my own airline. Whenever I wanted a concession of any kind I'd go to a certain official. If he refused, I'd take out my glass eye and put it on the desk in front of him. 'I have given my most valuable possession for your country,' I would say, 'and you refuse me this small thing!' The eye seemed to horrify him. He'd scream to me that if I would take it away I could have anything I wanted."

From the small beginning in Honduras, Yerex built up an airline network known as TACA. He and Lil were divorced, and in a short time he married the daughter of a high Central American government official. Later he sold TACA for several million dollars.

Pangborn's Western demonstration tour had started at Riverside, California. Expenses were met by carrying passengers, rather than calling on the parent corporation in New Jersey. The trip up the coast was revealing of aviation's growth. Where Pang had flown from grain fields and pastures there were now airports. Every small town seemed to have a plane or two. In Portland, Vance Breese was building airplanes designed by Jack Northrop. Tex Rankin was running one of the largest flying schools in the United States and buying planes by the carload. Boeing was expanding in Seattle. Los Angeles was the site of scores of airframe manufacturers. Airlines now had a network along the coast.

Back in San Diego, Pangborn received a wire.

COME EAST. MAKE IT FAST.

The New Standard Corporation had never made a profit. The collapse of the market had sent its stock to zero. With no prospect for the future, the officers closed the doors. Once again Pangborn had lost money on a project which at first had looked so promising.

He ordered one of the demonstration planes to Los Angeles, where it was turned over to the corporation's agents, Jack Frye and Paul Richter. The two later became officers of Trancontinental-Western Air better known by its initials "TWA" and still later to become Trans-World Airlines. Herndon flew the second demonstrator east.

The trip up and down the Pacific Coast had convinced Pangborn that people would still pay to fly around a field; that the old and tried advertising gimmicks would still work. Back in the east he said to Herndon:

"I think we can buy the old Empire Air Circus equipment pretty cheap. Empire has gone broke, along with us and about two hundred other aviation firms. How'd you like to go barnstorming?"

"I think it would be swell," Herndon replied.

Mrs. Alice Boardman, Herndon's mother, had often said to

Pang: "If you can find anything in which Hughie seems to be interested and you can fit him into your plans, I'd be glad to put money in it for him."

In New York Pangborn discussed the new proposal with Mrs. Boardman. She agreed that if it would get Hugh and his brother, Robert, out into the fresh air, away from Park Avenue and the neighboring night clubs, it was a sound investment.

Mrs. Boardman put up $10,000 and Pangborn drew an equal amount from that deposit he had made in the Lodi bank. Three of the Empire airplanes were purchased, together with a Packard limousine, a truck and various accessories. Once again Ed Churchill was induced to leave the newspaper and go on the road as advance man.

And so, persevering in his conviction that a flying circus would still pay (or maybe it was reluctance to admit defeat) Pangborn started still another barnstorming tour.

The Flying Fleet, the name chosen for the new operation, was the cleanest, tightest, most streamlined operation in barnstorming history. With the two partners flying, only one other pilot was needed. Churchill and Matty Kosvic were the advance men. Mechanics and parachute-jumpers were Mickey Efferson, Benny Matthews, Jerry Smith and Happy Johnson. Bookkeeper and ticket seller was goateed Tex Kimble. For a time the Packard was driven by Pang's brother, Percy, a national rifle and pistol champion and an expert jeweler.

Fighting bad weather which washed out several of its dates, the circus worked its way into the lower Rio Grande Valley which was enjoying a boom, despite the national depression. At Harlingen, Efferson, who had broken an arm in a parachute jump, was selling tickets, when an attractive skirt passed by. He turned over the booth to a total stranger and took off in pursuit of swivel-hips. The stranger sold $50 worth of tickets, then vanished with the loot.

"You'll have to make good that $50, or you're through," Pang told Mickey when he returned.

"Hell, if you do that to me, I'll quit."

"Okay, so you just quit."

Mickey, the man in the flying circus who would have been voted the least likely to succeed, went from managing marathon dances to flying in Central America. Finally, next to Yerex, he had the most successful career of all.

Pangborn and Hugh Herndon shortly after they had joined forces to create The Flying Fleet, their final circus venture.

In Pecos, in west Texas, the crew was about to shut down operations for the day when an automobile drove up. Its occupants approached Leon Echols, third pilot of the circus.

"How about a ride?" they asked.

Echols put two older people, two children and a beautiful girl into the front cockpit. His engine was still warm from the day's flying. He got a crank and took off. He forgot, however, that he had closed his Lunkenheimer, a fuel valve which allowed the flow of gasoline from the tanks in the upper wing to the carburetor. He gathered speed, pulled into the air, and while he was climbing the starved engine quit. Instead of landing straight ahead—the fundamental rule pounded into all pilots—he went into a sharp turn and stalled. The beautiful girl, who was Miss West Texas, was killed, the others injured. One of the older passengers died later.

The circus carried insurance costing thousands of dollars, but it couldn't collect for this accident. The airplanes, according to the Department of Commerce regulations, could carry only four passengers. Echols had loaded five. All bookings were canceled. The final settlement cost $5,000 in cash and legal fees. A $7,000 plane had been lost. Circus operations weren't stopped, but they came close to it.

Irony of the tragedy was that Herndon and Pangborn had fired Echols several days earlier for stunting passengers without parachutes. They had let him stay on until a relief pilot could arrive, bringing in Herndon's plane which he had stored at Teterboro.

Churchill called in from Yoakum where the circus was to dedicate an airport.

"There's no use booking this country," he told Pangborn. "A pilot named Perry Hutton had been through here in a three-engine Ford. He's featuring flight in a big skyliner, just like the airlines use. We're dead."

"Not quite," Pangborn replied. "Keep on going."

The big cabin jobs were tough competition. Because of the stock market crash and following depression, they could be purchased at panic prices. Tri-motored Fords and Fokkers, Wacos, Travelairs, Stinsons, all were available. Late 1929 and 1930 found Hutton, Clyde Ice, Jimmy Barwick, Harold Johnson, Nick Mamer and several others barnstorming with the cabin jobs. Pang and Herndon couldn't afford the big equipment themselves; all their money was tied up in the open New Standards.

In three years time, through 1930, more than 12,000 aircraft had been produced. Airlines, touching most of the major cities in the country, carried 374,935 passengers in 1930. Most of these passengers rode in multi-engine transports with heated cabins. Radio aids were being installed along the airways, which, at night, were also marked by rotating beacon lights which could be seen for miles.

As of January 1, 1931, there were 7,354 licensed pilots. Pangborn still carried his license, No. 240. Frank Hawks had flown coast-to-coast in 12 hours, 25 minutes. Forrest O'Brien and Dale (Red) Jackson had set an endurance record of 647 hours and 28 minutes.

Pangborn and Herndon struggled against the new competition and the latest developments in equipment until the end of February, 1931. The final gasp of The Flying Fleet was on the Palo Alto, California field. In thirteen months they had carried 121,000 passengers and had booked into nearly 100 cities in 36 states.

They had nothing to show for their efforts.

The New Standards were rolled into a hangar.

"We'll get them out and fly them again when this goddamn depression is over," Pangborn declared.

Instead, they were sold for hangar rent.

Pangborn recalled a ditty from his Army Air Service days:

"They gave us wings with which to fly
And then they took away the sky."

25

First Across the Pacific

IT WAS HARD for Pangborn to believe that the barnstorming days were over. In some 12 years of gypsy flying he had personally flown more than 100,000 passengers. He had operated from several hundred different towns and cities throughout the United States. His log book showed that he had accumulated more than 10,000 air hours.

Many of those hours had been routine and monotonous. A few had been frightening. Most had given him pleasure and satisfaction, the enjoyment he had always known he would find in the sky. They had made him a respected member of the tightly-knit flying fraternity. He had, indeed, looked at "the other side of the mountain," beyond new horizons.

Yet Pang had little to show in a material way for the years in the air. This despite the fact that the circus, of which he had been a full partner, had taken in several million dollars. There were scattered bank accounts, such as the one in Lodi, but he wasn't even sure of the amounts. As he contemplated the prosaic need of earning a living he knew that effort must embrace flying.

His thoughts went back to a conversation he had had with Bernt Balchen on Roosevelt Field in 1927. In May of that year three different planes were being readied for an attempt to cross the Atlantic. The prize was $25,000 offered by the Frenchman, Orteig, for the first New York-Paris non-stop flight. Of equal importance to the money was the fame and possible fortune which would result from the feat, if successful.

Waiting impatiently for suitable weather were Charles A. Levine and Clarence D. Chamberlin, Commander Richard E. Byrd and his pilots Bernt Balchen and Bert Acosta, and a loner, Charles Lindbergh.

Such an assemblage naturally attracted other fliers and among those closely watching the preparations on Long Island were Wiley Post and Pangborn. Post speculated beyond the Atlantic flight and talked to Balchen about his idea for an around-the-world attempt. Later Balchen said to Pangborn, "If Wiley doesn't try that flight we should do it ourselves."

Lindbergh's successful flight, and the fact that the two other planes also succeeded in crossing the ocean—Chamberlin landed in Germany, Byrd on the coast of France—gave impetus to plans for other long distance projects. Of those days Pangborn later said:

"Those flights were not foolhardy. We knew we had good equipment. Engines were reliable. Proper planning and attention to details, particularly navigation, were the keys to success."

Pang already had proved engine reliability to his own satisfaction. At Syracuse, New York, he had stayed in the air for 179 hours, seven full days plus 11 hours, in an attempt to set a new endurance record. On that occasion his plane had been refueled twice each day by another aircraft. On any long distance flight, however, refueling would be impossible. The plane itself would have to carry sufficient fuel to achieve the objective.

The Atlantic now offered little challenge. As early as 1919 it had been conquered when the United States Navy's NC-4 flying boat completed its flight in stages from Trepassy Bay, Newfoundland, to Horta, Spain. Then, in the same year, the Britishers Captain John Alcock and Lieutenant Arthur Whitten-Brown flew non-stop from St. Johns, Newfoundland, to Galway, Ireland, in a twin-engine Vickers Vimy bomber. Again in 1919 the Atlantic was conquered by the British dirigible R-34 in a flight from the Firth of Forth in Scotland to Mineola, Long Island. By the time Lindbergh made his spectacular solo flight the Atlantic had already been flown by nearly one hundred persons.

Thus it was that Pangborn went back to the idea implanted in 1927 by Bernt Balchen. Pang proposed to Herndon that they attempt to set an around-the-world record. It would be a spectacular achievement, lead to new recognition and open new business possibilities. The first record had been set in 1889 when Nellie Bly sped around the globe by ship and train in 72 days, six hours and 11 minutes. John Henry Mears, in 1913, halved Nellie's mark when he went around in 35 days, 21 hours and 36 minutes.

In 1924, four Army aircraft had set out from Seattle to circle the globe and six months later two of the original planes completed the flight. However, the record that Pangborn had in mind was that of the German Graf Zeppelin—twenty days, four hours, set in 1929.

Why had he chosen Herndon when Pang had so many more experienced friends in flying circles? Herndon had performed well with the Gates circus and later as a partner in the Flying Fleet. More important, he came from a wealthy family and financing the project was a major hurdle to be overcome.

The first step, after Herndon agreed enthusiastically to the proposal, was to form an organization and arrange the financial details. The RTW (Round-the-World) corporation was created with Herndon as president and Robert B. Heebner as manager. Again Pangborn accepted a secondary management role, though the project depended entirely on his skill.

A Bellanca monoplane was selected for its weight lifting capabilities. Herndon wrote a check for $100,000 to purchase the equipment and provide for the fuel and other supplies that would be needed. The funds were made available by Mrs. Boardman, Herndon's mother. His aunt also contributed $15,000 to the project.

In its March 21, 1931 issue the *New Yorker* magazine quoted Herndon as saying: "We will make the flight on three conditions. We will take no subscriptions from anybody. We will pay cash for the things we have to get, including gas and oil. Finally we will make the most careful preparations that have ever been made for a long distance flight."

The latter statement was in accord with Pangborn's strong conviction: careful planning and preparation, plus individual performance, would determine success or failure.

Headquarters of the RTW organization were set up in a New York

Bert Acosta, noted flyer, wishes Pangborn and Herndon good luck shortly before take-off on the global flight.

hotel suite. Pang was well aware that navigation would be vital as they crossed unfamiliar waters and land masses. Maps and charts, such as were available, were obtained through the state department. Interpreters were brought in to translate the foreign cartography.

In June, 1931, Pangborn wrote his mother:

"No doubt you have wondered why I haven't written before. As you know I came back here in March and things have been progressing slowly. Now they are shaping up and we are getting ready to go. When I arrived here I found the plane had a Wright J6 motor in it which would not be so hot for this particular trip. Finally I was able to persuade Hughie that we should have a Wasp 425 engine installed as it is one of the most powerful and dependable engines built. It burns more gas than the J6 and thus we will not have as long cruising range, but it will get us out of shorter fields than we would have been able to handle with the smaller engine.

"The route we plan is as follows: From New York we will follow the steamship route which goes directly east for about one thousand miles, then swings northeast to England. This avoids the icebergs and bad weather further north. It keeps us out of the fog and cold weather from Newfoundland, the route the other fliers are taking.

"We have given up the idea of flying straight across the Pacific as it is too near our margin of safety. Instead, after crossing Russia and Siberia we will go up to the Kamchatka Peninsula and along the Aleutian Islands, across Alaska and down through Canada to New York.

"The only other fliers planning round-the-world flights are Post and Gatty; the others are just trying non-stop long distance flights. Post and Gatty are flying a Lockheed, which is faster than our Bellanca, but not as dependable from short fields.

"Herndon went up to Albany on Saturday to see his girl. We made a test run down to Puerto Rico to give Hugh navigation experience. Bert Yancey went along as he has been instructing Hugh. We were the guests of Governor Theodore Roosevelt, Jr., for two days. He is in New York now and the other day invited me to lunch with Vincent Astor and others. Now don't worry as I don't look for any trouble, and if we have good luck on weather it will be ridiculously easy. Tell everyone hello. Love, Clyde."

Checking the proposed route Yancey observed that the shortest and fastest way would be straight across the Gulf of Alaska, from the mid-Aleutian chain, to the northern tip of the Queen Charlotte Islands. Pang replied: "Okay, that's the way we will go." Both Pang and Yancey had supreme faith in the Wasp engine, not only to lift an extremely heavy load, but to perform faultlessly under all conditions and for long periods.

Difficulty was encountered in obtaining permission from the Russians for the necessary landing in Moscow and the onward flight across eastern Russia and Siberia. As a last resort, the assistance of Senator Borah from Pangborn's home state of Idaho was requested. His intervention through the State Department resulted in the permits being granted.

As preparations went forward a number of other fliers were poised for various long-distance flights, as Pangborn indicated in the letter to his mother. They included Bernt Balchen in a tri-motor

Fokker, Roger Q. Williams in a single engine Emsco, Shirley Short in a Bellanca, Wiley Post and Harold Gatty in a Lockheed, Mr. and Mrs. Charles Healy Day in a sport plane of Day's design.

Still others were Ruth Nichols, Otto Hillig and Hoiegor Hoiriis, Russell Boardman and John Polando, and Vance Breese and John Henry Mears, who, like Pangborn and Herndon, were planning a round-the-world flight. This was the same Mears who had established a record in 1913. (Pang wasn't aware of the plan of Breese and Mears at the time he wrote his mother.)

Then in the last week of June, 1931, Wiley Post and Harold Gatty, in the Winnie Mae, made aviation history. Following essentially the same route as that planned by Pangborn and Herndon, they circled the globe in 8 days, 15 hours and 51 minutes, cutting the Graf Zeppelin time by 11 days and more. Now Pangborn and Herndon faced a double challenge; not only to make the world flight, but to do it in less time than Post and Gatty. Since the latter flew a Lockheed, which was faster than the Bellanca, Pang and Herndon would have to fly longer legs, spend less time on the ground.

Last minute details were myriad. Pang concentrated on the equipment and route-planning, leaving the business end to Herndon. In connection with the latter, Herndon presented a number of papers to Pang and asked him to sign them. Without reading, Pang casually affixed his signature. As usual, the business details of any enterprise were of secondary interest to him.

Some four weeks after the Post-Gatty flight, Pangborn and Herndon were ready. Present for the take-off were Herndon's mother and—a surprise—his wife. A society reporter had broken the story just the day before that Herndon and Mary Ellen Farley had married a few weeks earlier. The marriage had not been revealed to Pangborn, no doubt because they knew he would frown on it as an interference to the flight plans, as proved to be the case.

The take-off was being attempted from Roosevelt Field No. 1, separated from No. 2 by a drop-off of several feet. Pang held the plane, which had been named "Miss Veedol," at the end of the runway while he brought the engine up to full power, then he released the brakes. The Bellanca lumbered down the runway. Twenty—40—50 miles an hour. But it was not accelerating as fast as Pang wanted.

With the big red Bellanca poised at the end of the runway, the press gets final shots just before Pangborn and Herndon take-off on the first leg of their world flight.

It quickly became apparent that they would not have enough speed to get off the ground. And there wasn't sufficient runway remaining in which to stop the heavily loaded plane.

"Pull the dump valve" Pang ordered.

Released of part of its load, the plane staggered into the air, just cleared a hangar, and was nursed gently around the pattern to a landing. Only Pang's superb skill had averted a tragedy such as had overtaken the French flier, Rene Fonck, at the same spot. Failing to attain take-off speed, Fonck's plane plunged over the embankment and burst into flames. Two of the crew perished in the ensuing fire.

The Bellanca, after its brush with disaster, was moved to the slightly longer Roosevelt runway No. 2. There, refueled and re-checked, it joined the plane of Boardman and John Polando who were also ready to go.

On July 28 Boardman took off at 5:59 a.m., bound for ancient Constantinople—now Istanbul. Pangborn and Herndon followed at 6:18 on their proposed flight non-stop to England. Two airplanes in the air over the Atlantic, only minutes apart! Surprisingly the plane destined for the more southern objective was taking the more northern route. Pang was tracking more to the south in the hope of avoiding the storms and fog of the northern route.

Unfortunately, and inexplicably, the big red Bellanca encountered fog almost immediately and it was to persist all the way across the Atlantic. Having been up all the night before take-off supervising final preparations, Pangborn turned the controls over to Herndon after a few hours, gave him the heading and altitude, and promptly went to sleep. When he awoke he noted immediately that Herndon was ten degrees off course and had no idea how long he had flown the wrong heading. Pang estimated the length of his nap, assumed that Herndon had almost immediately deviated from the proper course, and corrected back toward the plotted heading.

Thirty hours passed. Pang was certain they must be over land. He found a hole in the clouds, circled, and came down to see green fields below which he identified as Ireland. On across St. George's Channel they were overtaken by dusk and Pang landed in a farmer's field. For a barnstormer who had picked out hundreds of untried landing spots, this was no great feat. By coincidence the farmer who first greeted them was named Herndon. He informed them that they were at Moylegrove in Pembrokeshire, Wales, then drove them to the Black Lion Inn at Cardigan. When they asked for rooms and some dinner they had considerable difficulty convincing the host at the Inn that they had just flown across the ocean from the United States.

Up early the next morning they took off and arrived at Croydon, outside London, at 8:15 a.m. On the way they had passed over the town of Pangborn! Pang hoped to refuel and be back in the air enroute to Moscow within an hour. However, Mrs. Boardman had cabled relatives in London to meet the plane. They came to the field, picked up Herndon and took off with him in their car.

As the hours went by Pang fumed. Here they were, trying to set a speed record, and valuable time was being lost while Herndon was making a social visit. Finally, completely exasperated, Pang entered the cockpit, started the engine, and was about to taxi out for take-off by himself when Hugh and his relatives dashed up. Thus was born another rift in what had started out as an ideal working partnership. The first had been Herndon's secret marriage, which accounted for Hugh's frequent absences during the trip-planning period and his lack of concentration on navigation studies.

They took off from Croydon at 2:13 p.m.—six hours lost on the ground—for Berlin where they landed at Templehof airport at 7:30 p.m. A brief stop for refueling and a bite to eat, then on to Moscow where they were nine hours and 58 minutes behind the time of Post and Gatty. On eastward they approached the Ural mountains. Terrific winds buffeted them as they fought for sufficient altitude for the crossing. More time was lost as they flew back and forth paralleling the mountains before they finally skimmed through a pass.

East of Novosibirsk, where they had paused briefly to refuel, Herndon—at the controls while Pang napped—again lost the way. When he awoke, Pang landed at a village where the one resident who could speak English told them they were in Mongolia and pointed the general direction to Chita.

Back on course after more hours lost they left Chita at 5:30 p.m. for Khabarovsk, which would be their last stop in Siberia. Foul weather persisted all through the night and they arrived at the far-eastern city in a deluge. The runway was several inches of mud and clay. When they touched down the tires hydroplaned and, with the brakes practically useless, they slid off the end of the runway into deeper mud where they mired. After a day of waiting out the storm, ropes were fixed to the landing gear and several hundred volunteers helped pull the plane back onto the runway and to a hangar. There the muddy and somewhat bedraggled ship was cleaned.

Now more than 27 hours behind Post-Gatty time and with no possibility of being able to take off from the boggy field, they were forced to abandon the speed attempt.

At a strategy meeting, and after conferring with their New York office, it was decided that they would continue to Japan when the field dried. From there they would attempt a non-stop flight to the United States in quest of the $25,000 prize offered by the Japanese newspaper *Asahi Shimbun* for the first such flight.

Pangborn cabled the editor of the *Japanese Times,* an English language newspaper in Tokyo, asking them to wire the direction and distance of Tachikawa airport from Tokyo, emphasizing that he had no maps or charts. He also asked that the American embassy file a landing application with the Japanese Aviation Bureau.

Meantime in Kharbarovsk the field had dried. Although the necessary information had not arrived Pangborn decided to take off before another storm might strike. A message from the *Times* was delivered shortly after the take-off. It gave the requested directional information and said that the Japanese Aviation Bureau would grant the landing permit on application from the American embassy.

On the comparatively short hop—for them—to Japan, they flew over the Taugaru Strait to Aomori prefecture, where the Japanese said later there were naval installations, and then along the coast to Tokyo Bay. Both a still and a 16-mm movie camera had been included among their equipment. Intrigued by the picturesque Japanese landscape, Herndon shot film with both cameras. They landed first at Haneda airport, a new installation between Tokyo and Yokahama, which was not yet open for traffic. There they were directed to Tachikawa airport, where authorities boarded the plane and demanded landing papers. When the documents could not be produced the two Americans were escorted from the plane and turned over to the police. Pang readily admitted that they carried cameras and had taken pictures. After brief preliminary questioning they were placed under house restriction at the famed Frank Lloyd Wright-designed Imperial hotel in downtown Tokyo.

"We were arraigned on three counts" Pangborn related later. "That we had flown over Japan without a permit, that we had flown over fortified areas and that we had photographed those areas. True, we didn't have the flight permit with us, but we had assumed it would be routine for our embassy to arrange it. As to flying over fortified areas and taking pictures, we were just tourists taking what we thought were pretty landscape shots."

When the fliers and their friends in America asked the American embassy to intercede for them, it at first said the fliers had violated the laws of Japan and that it could do nothing.

"We weren't jailed, but we were restricted in our movements," Pangborn said. "We had to be escorted everywhere and were subjected to endless questioning. Most of it was ridiculous. For example, in searching the plane, the police found a few pounds of rice. They couldn't understand why we carried it. It was impossible to make clear that this was part of our emergency food supply in case we should have been forced down in a remote area.

"It was likewise impossible to get over to them that it would have been very stupid to fly more than half way around the world, get lost, bog down in the mud, take pictures of restricted areas, and then land in the very country allegedly being spied on.

"And we couldn't get through to the American Ambassador. Every time we tried to contact him we were told he was out playing golf. If he had been on the job we would have been released in no time. It was only when my mother got Senator Borah to again intercede for us, this time direct with the Japanese ambassador in Washington D.C., that we were released."

When Pangborn and Herndon revealed their plan to attempt the Japan-U.S. flight—their only reason for coming to Japan—they were given reluctant permission, but at the same time were told that they would be allowed only one attempt at take-off.

They would not be the first to challenge the broad Pacific in non-stop flight. On August 18, 1929, Harold Bromley, attempting a take-off from a military field near Tacoma, Washington, cracked up when his Lockheed veered from a launching ramp. On August 12, 1931, Bob Wark was forced down at Vancouver, British Columbia, approximately 100 miles from his starting point. These attempts assaulted the difficult east-to-west crossing against the prevailing winds.

The next year Bromley teamed with Gatty for an attempt at the west-to-east crossing: Japan to the U.S. After surveying numerous possible take-off sites, all of which they found to be too short, they finally selected Sabishiro Beach, a smooth sandy stretch slightly more than 8,000 feet long, located some 200 miles north of Tokyo. On September 15, 1931 they made a successful take-off, but were forced to return by a balky engine after being in the air for 24 hours.

Two persistent chaps were Harold Jones and Reg Robbins. Attempting a Seattle-to-Japan flight they were forced down at Nome, Alaska. On a second attempt they were again forced down, this time at Fairbanks. Apparently growing tired of Seattle-Alaska flights, they gave up further attempts.

On June 1, 1931, Thomas Ash failed on an attempted take-off from Sabishiro. Still another attempt was that of Moyle and Allen on September 7, 1931. They got off successfully from the beach at Sabishiro, but were forced down on the Kamchatka Peninsula. They took off again only to be forced down once more, this time on an uninhabited island. It was a week before they were finally rescued.

Getting back to Pangborn and Herndon, on September 2, 1931, the Japanese custom agents finally released the Bellanca to them. Even then the permit for the short flight from Tokyo to Sabishiro was held up for several days. When it did come through it required that they fly 50 miles out at sea on the 200-mile flight north.

Pang had been busy planning the trans-Pacific flight and working out technical details during their involuntary stay in Tokyo. He also prepared charts of the route from such information as was available. His early experience as a civil engineer proved valuable in this project.

"We determined that to make the flight we would have to take off with the heaviest wing loading we had ever attempted with the Ballanca," Pang said later. "Even then it was marginal that we would have enough fuel to take us the approximately 4,500 miles to the U.S. west coast even at the most economical cruising speed. Studying the problem I calculated that we could increase our speed approximately 15 miles per hour if we could rid ourselves of the drag of the fixed landing gear. On a 40-hour flight that would be the equivalent of adding 600 miles to our range, and that might make the difference between success and failure."

Once this bold step was decided upon Pang designed special sleeves and coiled springs to release the gear. These would fit on the inner ends of the wheel axles. The outer ends would be drilled and pins inserted. From these pins cables would run to the cabin. Pulling the pins would spring the wheels free and release the landing gear struts, it was hoped.

Some of the work, including installation of a steel plate on the belly of the aircraft as a landing skid, was accomplished by Pangborn while under Japanese escort at the hangar where the plane was held. Necessary machine shop work was done in secret by American friends.

Several of these friends went north to Sabishiro to assist the fliers in their final preparations. Among them was a chap named Evans and a girl, apparently a far east correspondent for several American language newspapers, identified in Pang's notes only as "Fritz." Pang surveyed the beach foot by foot and noted that a pile of drift logs marked the end of the useful runway. Inspection of the take-off ramp used in previous attempts—a structure designed to give an airplane initial acceleration—indicated that it would have to be altered to fit the tread of the Bellanca.

Last minute installation of the release pins and wires on the landing gear became apparent to Japanese observers at the beach. Then on Friday, September 30, when heavy crosswinds prevented their planned take-off, the two fliers were in fear that the unusual work on the plane might cause the Japanese authorities to cancel their take-off permit.

"However, the Aviation Bureau closed on Saturday, so it was too late for them to hold one of their famous conferences," Pangborn noted. "And no Japanese could take action on his own."

At last, early in the morning of October 1, 1931, all was ready for the hazardous, one-time take-off attempt. The regular wing tanks, plus a special tank which had been installed in the fuselage, held 915 gallons of fuel. In addition there was 45 gallons of oil. Total take-off weight would be 8,920 pounds.

Pang wore Japanese-type coveralls and two pairs of heavy wool socks, no shoes. Herndon wore heavy slacks, a flight jacket and street oxfords. "Fritz," the newspaper girl, had prepared food for them—sandwiches, cheese, fried chicken and very hot tea. In her excitement she had forgotten to put in the breasts and thighs of the chicken. All they had were wings and backs.

At the last moment it was discovered that the charts which Pang had prepared were missing. For weeks the fliers had been assailed by the radical Black Dragon society. Without proof, they nevertheless suspected that the society was responsible for loss of the charts.

On the ramp, holding with the brakes, Pang went through all his checks, and finally ran the engine up to 1700 rpm. When he released the brakes the plane lumbered down the ramp and on to the sand of the beach. From the corner of his eye Pang saw his friends waving. There was no time to wave in return. Slowly, ever so slowly, the plane gained speed. Forty . . . fifty miles an hour. One mile and the speed was only up to sixty. Pang had calculated they would need nearly ninety for take-off. The performance curves for the plane did not anticipate such load as was aboard, consequently the performance figures did not go that far.

At a mile and one-half Pang rocked the ship from wheel to wheel, attempting to break it loose from the friction of gravity on the sand. Finally, less than 200 yards from the logs at the end of the beach, the Bellanca became unstuck and struggled into the air. Pang felt as though he had physically lifted it from the sand.

"I was determined to get off, or pile into those logs," he said later. "We had permission for only the one attempt and in no way was I going to spend any more time in Japan."

Barely holding above stalling speed, the controls sloppy, and the plane wallowing, Pang continued straight ahead for several miles, gaining only a few feet of altitude per minute. Finally he dared to make a cautious, very wide turn back to a heading of 72 degrees true, which he had calculated would take them up to the Aleutian chain, across the Gulf of Alaska, down to the Queen Charlotte Islands, off the coast of British Columbia and thence to the United States. That is, the route appears "up" and "down" on a flat map. On a globe it becomes a straight line, hence the constant heading.

When the Pacific flight was decided upon, after abandonment of the round-the-world effort, the potential for three prize money awards was part of the motivation. The first was the $25,000 being offered by the Tokyo *Asahi Shimbun,* one of Japan's largest newspapers. The second was the $25,000 which they understood was being offered by a Texan, Colonel Easterwood, for the first one-stop Japan-Texas flight. Finally there was yet another $25,000 offered by the City of Seattle for the first Japan-Seattle flight. The latter was scrubbed from their plans before take-off, for they had learned that its terms required departure or landing within 50 miles of Tokyo and 10 miles of Seattle. No airport within that limit of Tokyo had a runway long enough to permit their take-off with the required fuel load.

On course, and slowly gaining altitude, Pang decided to take the vital, non-reversible step of dropping the landing gear. So, some three hours out from Sabishiro, the wires were pulled and the pins released. The wheels and part of the landing gear dropped free. However, Pang was alarmed to see that two struts had not come loose. In a belly

This impressive shaft on Sabishiro beach, Japan, marks the take-off spot of Pangborn's non-stop Pacific flight. Standing in front of the monument is Dr. Kimura, noted Japanese aeronautical expert.

landing they might punch through the fuselage. This was a problem to be attended to later. The immediate problem was to hold course and continue the climb through the clouds in the hope of reaching clear air above.

During the enforced stay in Japan, Pang had discovered that the documents he had signed so hurriedly in New York provided all proceeds of the flight were first to go to Herndon to repay for the plane and other funds provided. Pang would receive nothing until Herndon was fully recompensed. It was hardly a 50-50 partnership arrangement, for Pangborn was contributing something of more value than Herndon's money—his flying skill. Thus the rift which had started with Herndon's secret marriage and his inept navigation and piloting, was now broadened to the point where the two men were scarcely speaking, though they gave no outward evidence of this.

"We started to pick up ice just as night fell," Pang wrote in his notes. "It was so cold the water in our canteens, and even our hot tea, froze. Finally we got on top at 14,000 feet and the moon came up about four hours after sunset. On the course I had plotted our first major fix was to be a volcano in the Aleutian Islands. I was delighted to see it loom directly below us. Following the compass, with the north star as a check, we were holding to our course."

Shortly after coming out on top of the cloud layer at 14,000 feet, Pang performed a fantastic feat. He turned the controls over to Herndon and climbed out on the broad wing strut of the Bellanca. Holding on with one hand in the 100 miles-an-hour bitter cold wind, knowing the ocean was thousands of feet below, he freed the two landing gear struts which had hung up, and saw them drop away clear. His many years of wing-walking experience had proved valuable.

One of Herndon's few responsibilities on the flight was to work the hand wobble pump which transferred fuel from the fuselage tank to the main wing tank, whence it was fed to the engine. Twice he let the main tank run dry whereupon the engine stopped. From 15,000 feet Pang dived almost vertically to windmill the heavy propeller and restart the engine while Herndon worked frantically to correct the error.

Below were the wind-lashed waters of the Gulf of Alaska, among the roughest in the world. Off to the left was the Alaska mainland with its peaks and glaciers crowding down to the sea, an unhospitable area for ship or plane.

"That water looked awfully black and awfully near when I pulled out at fifteen hundred feet," Pang wrote.

Back at altitude the hours crept by . . .20 . . .30. Hours without sleep. Finally the north tip of the Queen Charlottes was sighted and Pang knew they were right on course. Ahead, in a few hours, lay the testing task of landing the plane on its belly, without damage, so that a new landing gear could be attached and the flight continued to Texas in quest of the Easterbrook prize. In preparation for the landing Pang decided he should get a bit of sleep. His instructions to Herndon were:

"Just hold this course and altitude. When you see the lights of a large city, wake me up, that will be Vancouver, British Columbia."

Herndon awakened him some time later. It was two o'clock in the morning. They had been in the air nearly forty hours. Pang took over and through a rift in the clouds saw that they were only a thousand feet above the crest of 14,000-foot Mount Rainier; a mountain which he knew was some sixty miles south and east of Seattle. Herndon had missed both Vancouver and the American city.

Meantime at Wenatchee, on the banks of the Columbia River in eastern Washington, some twenty or thirty people had gathered at the small airport on a bluff above the city. Among them were Mrs. Opal Pangborn, Clyde's mother; his brother and sister-in-law, Mr. and Mrs. Percy Pangborn; a reporter for *The Daily World,* the local newspaper, and a half-dozen other optimists who dared to think the fliers would actually succeed and might land at their field.

A brief news flash had advised of the take-off from Sabishiro on Saturday. Then on Sunday James Manenias, a ham radio operator at False Pass in the Aleutians, reported that he had heard a plane overhead in the fog. The hours dragged slowly for those holding vigil on the ground. Shortly after midnight on Monday morning there was a vague report of an airplane heard over Seattle.

The night was cold, below freezing. The few gathered at the airport crowded around the heater in the small airport office. Clyde's mother, however, was outside in the family car. At four o'clock the local newspaper reporter suggested she come inside where it was warmer.

"No," she said. "I'm going to take a nap. They won't be here until seven o'clock!"

Confidence! Ice cold nerve! The mother who didn't panic when the three year old lad walked a four-story window sill. It was obvious where Clyde and his brother Percy both got their *sang froid*.

In the air Pang was concentrating on the next major step in their over-all plan. That was to land at some airport where new landing gear could be installed. If they could reach Boise, Idaho, they would also have established a new non-stop distance record, besting the New York-Istanbul record of Boardman and Polando.

Eastward toward Idaho the flight continued in the final night darkness. But that area was socked in solid with fog. Even back in his own country Pang was meeting this persistent nemesis. He probed toward Spokane. No luck, solid undercast. Back west and south toward Pasco. More fog. Fuel was running low. Numbing fatigue assailed both men. Pang decided to try Wenatchee. He was fairly sure it would be without fog. He knew the field well. And his mother and brother lived there.

Thus it was that a few minutes after seven o'clock a big red airplane swept low over the hills to the east and dived toward the airport. Those waiting in the small office dashed outside at the first sound of the plane's engine. They were surprised and uncertain, for they had expected the plane, if it came at all, would come from the west, from toward the Pacific, not from the east.

Pang buzzed the field, only a few feet off the ground, looking it over carefully, then pulled up to go around and dump the remainder of his fuel. The wheelless plane somehow seemed vulgarly nude to those below.

On the single phone line from the airport the local reporter was describing the scene and the action to the downtown newspaper office and from there it was being relayed to the wire services on the West Coast and in New York.

While the newsman was describing how Pang was dumping fuel in preparation for the landing, a voice broke in on the phone:

"This is the New York operator. I have a call for Mr. Clyde Pangborn."

"Lady, he isn't here."

"How soon do you expect him?"

"Look! He's just in from Japan. He's overhead in an airplane. It doesn't have any wheels. He has to make a landing on his belly!"

"Have him call operator two, sev-un, nigh-un when he arrives."

There was a girl with romance and adventure in her soul and 100 per cent devotion to the prescribed operating procedures.

To the south of the city the plane was squared away for the runway and starting to descend. Herndon was back on top of the auxiliary fuel tank to help hold the tail down during the anticipated landing slide. Pang fish-tailed violently, slowing the plane to a near stall. Over the end of the runway he cut the switch, hoping to stop the propeller in a horizontal position. Unfortunately it windmilled to the vertical.

He held off, just skimming the ground, the nose high. Then the Bellanca was on its belly and sliding forward. A cloud of dust at first

The wheelless "Miss Veedol" just before touchdown at Wenatchee, Washington, after 41-hour flight across the Pacific from Japan.

obscured the plane from those watching, amazement on their faces. The tail tipped upward, teetered, then fell back and to one side as the plane slithered to a stop. The propeller tip had dug into the ground, causing the tail to flip up, despite Pang's best efforts.

As the dust settled the plane seemed to nestle down like a wounded bird. There wasn't a sound from the onlookers. Some started to run hesitantly toward the plane as though afraid of what they might find. All the way from Japan. Across the Pacific. And now?

The fuselage door on the right side opened. A movement inside the plane. Out slid one man—then another. One had a slight cut over his right eye. Herndon had been hit by a flying oil can when the plane nosed up. He pressed a handkerchief to his bleeding forehead. Pangborn looked at the underside of the plane.

First to greet the bleery eyed, unshaven, rather tattered but

The Pangborn-Herndon plane after its wheelless landing at Wenatchee, Washington, following its 41-hour non-stop flight across the Pacific from Japan.

smiling fliers were Pangborn's mother and his brother, Percy. A brief hug and a handshake for both of the men.

The small town of Wenatchee—some 17,000 inhabitants—went wild. Hundreds of cars tried to get to the airport on the steep one-way road up the bluff. Several out-of-town reporters, in Wenatchee on the long chance that the fliers might land there, were caught downtown. One photographer, trapped half way up the hill and seeing the plane circling to land, abandoned his car and raced for the runway, which he reached just as the plane came over the threshold. With a fine case of buck fever he shook so violently that he missed the shot entirely.

One of the most welcome persons at the field was a representative of *Asahi,* who with inordinate luck had picked Wenatchee as the most

Pangborn and Herndon just after skidding their plane to a stop on its belly after the Pacific flight. Greeting them are Pang's mother, Mrs. Opal Pangborn, and his brother Percy and sister-in-law.

likely landing place. The fliers were hardly on the ground before he presented them with a check for $25,000.

The Pangborn family, with the two fliers, started for town. Percy took a circuitous route over wheat fields and through barbed wire fences to avoid the tie-up on the one road. Hot baths, breakfast, clean clothes and sleep were uppermost in the minds of the exhausted men.

As the men were eating an Associated Press dispatch from Dallas came in. It quoted Colonel Easterbrook as saying that Pangborn and Herndon were not eligible for his prize; that he had reserved the right to select the fliers who would try for it. Pangborn did a fair job of old-fashioned country cussing when he heard the unwelcome news.

Seattle, which had surrounded its offer with almost impossible conditions and later had withdrawn it entirely, now clasped the fliers as fellow townsmen. A civic parade and a formal banquet were arranged. A large department store paid for the privilege of displaying the "Miss Veedol." The wings were taken off and the plane was trucked to Seattle. After the two-day display it was moved to Boeing Field where new landing gear was attached, so that the fliers could continue to New York for another civic welcome being planned there.

Following the brief stay in Seattle the fliers flew on to New York. With an eye to good public relations, Edward Bernays, the project public relations man, had prepared a statement which Herndon delivered at the civic reception.

"As far as Japan is concerned, we were treated splendidly," he said. "Of course we got a lot of publicity over our difficulties a month ago, but that is all ironed out. Unfortunately we did not get publicity about the friendliness displayed toward us after the difficulties were cleared up.

"And as to paying a fine and being detained is concerned, I don't blame Japan a bit. It was a result of our flying over fortifications without a proper permit and largely a matter of a dispute between two newspapers, one of which had obtained our story from a syndicate and another which wanted our story. As I say, the misunderstanding has long since been cleared up and I would like to emphasize the wonderful treatment accorded us by the Japanese people."

Prior to the take-off from Japan Mrs. Boardman, without explanation, had fired F. Darius Benham, original publicity man for the venture. In New York, on learning of this action, Pang wrote:

"Dear Freddy. I want you to know that I am aware of the treatment accorded you by Herndon and his mother, and that I had no part in it whatever."

And so, still another crack in the relationship. In fact, it had grown to a giant gap. Of the $25,000 Asahi prize, Pang received less that $2,500. Herndon kept the rest under terms of the documents Pang had hastily signed in New York back in July at the start of the adventure. And, of course, Herndon still retained ownership of the plane. Going over the signed documents with his brother in Seattle, Pang had also discovered that he was barred for a full year from making any personal appearances, endorsing any product, or doing any other kind of promotion that might be related to the flight.

The Bellanca was subsequently sold to Dr. Leon Pisculli and renamed "The American Nurse." With William Ulbright and Edna Newcomer, a practicing nurse, the Doctor set out on an attempt to fly the Atlantic to Italy. The plane and its passengers were lost at sea, somewhere south of the British Isles.

With sale of the aircraft and his lion's share of the prize money, Herndon was fully recompensed for his monetary contribution to the world flight. Pangborn for his exceptional flying, mechanical and navigation skills, got hardly anything from what he understood was to be a full partnership.

Though monetary benefits were not to come Pang's way, he did receive a singular honor when he was awarded the Harmon trophy—most prestigious of aviation awards—for 1931. The presentation was made in New York with the elite of aviation present. It was rather ironic that, while Pang was placed in the seat of honor at the head table, Herndon was "well below the salt," the two gentlemen on either side of him unable to converse in English.

Although the split between Pangborn and Herndon had been known for some time by their intimates and had been hinted at in the press, the first open disclosure occurred in Albany, New York. There the *Times Union* on December 22, 1931, a little more than two months after the Pacific flight, carried a headline which read: HERNDON INCOMPETENT SAYS PANGBORN.

The story went on to quote Pang as saying: "In this flight, Herndon was to be the navigator and I was to be the pilot. He was supposed to have studied navigation for months before our flight, and so far as he let the world know, he was qualified to undertake this task. But as a matter of fact Herndon was spending all his time courting Mary Ellen Farley of Lauderville. On the flight Herndon was more of a passenger than a pilot. Out of the more than 200 hours we were in the air, Herndon flew at most ten of those hours. And as to navigation, he knew nothing about it."

It was hardly in character for Pangborn to have made such a statement. In all his years of unpleasant relationship with Van Gates, he had never expressed criticism of his partner to others. His frustration and anger precipitated by Herndon's cavalier actions must have been great.

It is worth mentioning, however, that Herndon eventually attained sufficient experience to qualify for an airline job. He flew for T.W.A. during the war years and was later posted to Cairo, Egypt, where he died of a stroke in 1950.

For Pangborn the Pacific flight was the paradox of another success-failure. The Gates circus had been the greatest of its day. It had earned millions, and then had quietly folded in Florida. There had been the tight, efficient operation of The Flying Fleet and another demise without profit. And now, the disappointment of the aborted round-the-world attempt counter-pointed by the successful Pacific flight with world acclaim, but little else to show for it.

There had been, however, over the years, riches of a special kind . . . the riches of flight. The thousands of hours of pure joy in the air. The awareness that he was a part of an infant, but growing industry. The friendship of his fellow fliers who recognized and respected his talents.

Now, at 35, he must still look to the future, must continue to assuage that ever-present hunger for the sky.

Pangborn took stock of his situation. Thirty-five years old. Unmarried, no roots, limited finances. The country deep in a depression. Aviation, too, depressed; temporarily set back in its growth. And he had unwittingly signed papers effectively enjoining him from capitalizing in any way on the Pacific flight.

His brother Percy had purchased a ranch in a valley of the Cascade mountains of Washington and had placed it in Clyde's name.

The east slope of the Cascades with their Ponderosa pines, lakes and swift creeks and rivers, are a counterpart of the Idaho mountains and waters where Clyde had grown up.

Percy urged his brother to come west and settle down. He proposed that they work the ranch together, hunt, prospect the surrounding hills, fish the streams and lakes. It would be a return to that idyllic early life in Idaho.

The attraction of the mountains and forest was strong. But the lure of the propeller's blur, of feet on rudder, stick in hand, the unrestricting dimensions of the sky, were stronger. No, his future would not be earth-bound.

The years 1932 and 1933 found Pang engaged in the prosaic routine of earning a living. He delivered aircraft to South America. When an overnight express service was started between New York and Los Angeles, he flew the inaugural flight and continued to fly the service for four months.

In the spring of 1933 Pang returned to Wenatchee, Washington, terminus of his Pacific flight, to visit his mother and brother and sister-in-law. The easy informality of the small town appealed to him—the citizenry respected his privacy—and he was thoroughly relaxed.

The author of this book was fortunate enough to be invited on a picnic with the family into the Grand Coulee, ancient bed of a mighty river which was formed when the ice cap melted. At the head of the Coulee, several hundred feet below, the mighty Grand Coulee dam backs up the Columbia River in a 150-mile long lake to the Canadian border.

Both Percy Pangborn and his wife were repeat national champions at both pistol and rifle shooting. So it was natural that an assortment of guns went along with us on the picnic and that targets were set up for practice shooting.

Picking up a "45" from the arsenal Pang said, "The last time I saw that gun, Gates emptied it at me." Then he told of the incident in Easton when Gates had swung on him from behind, breaking his jaw, and then had seized the gun and emptied its six shots at his partner.

26

The World's Greatest Air Race

EARLY IN 1934 Pangborn was slated to fly a specially built Gee Bee Super Sportster in the upcoming MacRobertson race from England to Australia. The backing failed to materialize, however, and Jacqueline Cochran took over the unfinished airplane as a back-up entry in the event her supercharged Northrop Gamma developed problems. Thereupon, Pangborn threw in with the flamboyant Roscoe Turner who had arranged to lease a brand new Boeing transport from United Air Lines as his entry. Pangborn and Reeder Nichols were on Turner's payroll as co-pilot/navigator and radio operator respectively. The 11,325-mile event promised to be the race of the century.

The Australian chocolate manufacturer, Sir MacPherson Robertson, had put up a total of $75,000 in prizes and a gold cup for the three-continent race. Both military and civilian aircraft were eligible. Awards were to be made in two categories: open speed and handicap.

Turner had picked the Boeing 247 because of its range. There were faster planes in the race, but the Boeing could fly longer stages without refueling. The 247 was America's first twin-engined, low-wing, all-metal passenger transport. It featured a retractable landing gear, something of a novelty at that time, and had a top speed of 180 m.p.h. It set the pace for airliners to follow and sixty of the revolutionary aircraft were ordered by United Air Lines.

Turner took delivery of the aircraft direct from the production

Flight International photo.

Pangborn, Reeder Nichols, and Roscoe Turner just before departing Mildenhall Aerodrome for Australia.

line. It was a D-model, the first to fly, and differed from its predecessors in having the new 550-hp geared and supercharged Wasps with Hamilton-Standard controllable-pitch propellers. At altitude it could be expected to give a cruising speed of nearly 200 m.p.h. Long-chord cowlings and a swept back windshield helped boost performance and distinguished it from its forebearers.

Fred B. Collins, Boeing's sales manager at that time, recalls Turner's visit. "Roscoe was to stay at my house and he had that pet lion cub, Gilmore, with him. When I picked him up after a test hop he put the lion in the back seat of my car and we started for town. I was stopped at a traffic light when that goddamned lion started licking the back of my neck. It startled me so that I let out the clutch and we shot through the cross traffic narrowly missing several cars. A lion's tongue is about as rough as a rasp."

After Pang joined Turner they flew the Boeing to Los Angeles and then to New York. There the plane was loaded on the tennis deck of the *S.S. Washington*. Due to lack of equipment, it could not be off-loaded at Southampton, so they continued on to France. More complications developed when the French, rather unsportingly, demanded a bond of $20,000 before allowing the Boeing to be unloaded at Le Havre. Inasmuch as the airplane was in transit it had been assumed that they would be allowed to fly it to England without paying customs, but the French were adamant. The problem was solved, however, by arranging a transfer from the *Washington* to a sea-going lighter, which carried the Boeing back to Southampton without its touching French soil.

Although the Boeing was equipped with extra fuel tanks raising its capacity to 1,125 gallons and the range to something like 2,300 miles, the Race Committee ruled against full utilization of the tankage. The rules specified that only the amount allowed by the certifying agency—in this case the U.S. Civil Aeronautics Bureau—would be permitted. That was 950 gallons, but when the tanks were filled the Boeing was found to be some 180 lbs overweight. A drop in temperature, increasing the density of the fuel, plus the slightly greater weight of British fuel, combined to rob the Americans of a further forty gallons.

"That looks bad," Pangborn told his English friends, "because it means we won't be able to fly nonstop between the longest control points as planned." They had counted on the extra range to overcome the speed advantage of other entries, particularly the custom-built DeHavillands and the Dutch Pander high-speed mailplane.

Turner and Pangborn were not the only entries to have their fuel reduced. The Irishman, Col. James Fitzmaurice, was barred from carrying a full load in his specially built Bellanca. The reduced load meant a range penalty of 1,000 miles. Fitzmaurice argued futilely that another Bellanca, Pangborn and Herndon's, had already flown the Atlantic and the Pacific nonstop and had taken off with greater loads than proposed for the MacRobertson airplane.

Originally there had been over sixty entries from a dozen nations,

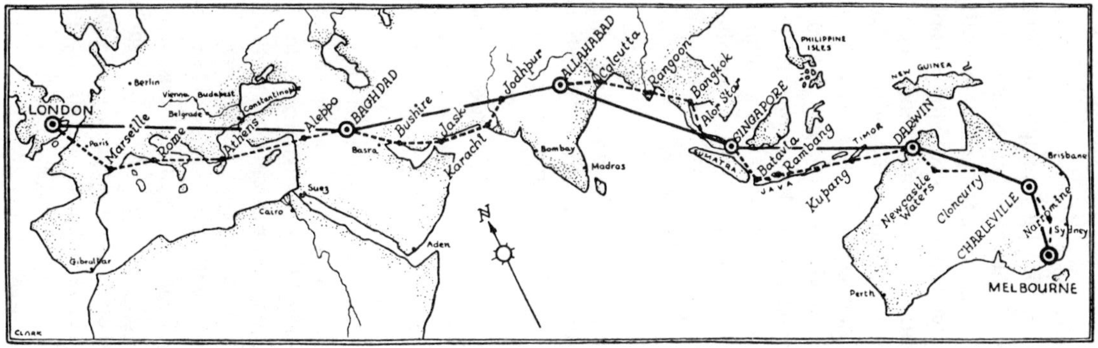

GREAT CIRCLE DISTANCES FOR SCRATCH RACE.—Mildenhall—Baghdad, 2,530 miles,—Allahabad, 2,300 miles,—Singapore, 2,210 miles,—Darwin, 2,084 miles,—Charleville, 1,389 miles,—Melbourne, 787 miles,—Total, 11,300 miles.

HANDICAP COURSE.—Mildenhall—Marseille, 652 miles,—Rome, 384 miles,—Athens, 654 miles,—Aleppo, 751 miles,—Baghdad, 450 miles (2,891 miles) :—Bushire, 486 miles,—Jask, 485 miles,—Karachi, 584 miles,—Jodhpur, 384 miles,—Allahabad, 542 miles (2,481 miles) :—Calcutta, 462 miles,—Rangoon, 639 miles,—Bangkok, 362 miles,—Alor Star, 533 miles,—Singapore, 409 miles (2,405 miles) :—Batavia, 570 miles,—Rambang, 682 miles,—Kupang, 495 miles,—Darwin, 511 miles (2,258 miles) :—Newcastle Waters, 384 miles,—Cloncurry, 514 miles,—Charleville, 536 miles (1,434 miles) :—Narromine, 420 miles,—Melbourne, 425 miles (845 miles),—Total, 12,314 miles.

Route of the MacRobertson Race.

with an assortment of surplus military, commercial airliners and small, single-engine private planes. However, only twenty actually appeared on the starting lineup. The favored team, comprising C.W.A. Scott and Tom Campbell-Black, was equipped with a crimson DeHavilland Comet, one of three such entries specially built for the race.

A race within the race developed when a Netherlands team selected a Douglas DC-2, rival of the Boeing 247, as its entry. It was flown by Capt. K.D. Parmentier, chief pilot of K.L.M., and J.J. Moll. In addition to its normal crew of three, the DC-2 carried three paying passengers, one being Thea Rasche, the famous German aviatrix. For three-fourths of the way Parmentier would be flying his regular K.L.M. route from the Netherlands to Batavia.

Starting positions were determined by lot. The husband and wife team of Capt. James Mollison and Amy Johnson, flying one of the

Flight International photo.

Pangborn and Turner taxiing the Boeing 247 out to start the MacRobertson Race.

Comets, was the first across the starting line at Mildenhall Aerodrome, 65 miles northeast of London. Pangborn and Turner were second off. Just before departure they presented a model of the 247D to the then Prince of Wales, the same Prince of Wales who had been amused by Pangborn's wing-walking at San Diego in 1920. The Prince, whose destiny it was to reign briefly as Edward VIII, was himself an avowed flying enthusiast and a licensed pilot.

In addition to having their fuel supply reduced, the Americans could not find aeronautical charts of the revised route they were forced to take. Ordinary tourist maps were available, however, and these had to suffice. Pangborn, the navigator, plotted a course to Athens which led directly over the Matterhorn, a check point they could hardly miss. Crossing France, the Americans were on top of clouds, but the towering pinnacle jutting through the fleece confirmed the accuracy of their flying. The weather cleared as the Boeing crossed the north of Italy, then headed down the east coast of the Adriatic and across Albania and Greece.

The Boeing landed at Athens behind the K.L.M. team, which had overtaken them somewhere enroute. At Athens they learned that Jackie Cochran was one of several forced down on the first day of the race. The next leg, across Turkey to Baghdad—again over clouds—was flown at 12,000 feet. In Baghdad the native ground crews were intrigued with the all-metal Boeing; they could walk on it almost anywhere and slide down the wing. The English planes with which they were familiar were fabric or plywood-covered and walking on them was strictly forbidden.

From Baghdad to Karachi the plotted course led across the wastelands of the Persian Desert. The Boeing's twin Wasps droned their paean of power across 1,300 miles of nothing but sand and barren, desolate mountains. At Karachi the Americans found that the Mollisons were abandoning the race because of engine trouble.

The next leg, Karachi to Allahabad in north central India, nearly proved disastrous. "I had been at the controls while Turner slept," Pangborn recounted afterwards. "Roscoe awoke after a good sleep and took over the controls. I gave him the course heading and told him we would be in Allahabad at 6:20 o'clock. Some two hours later I awakened to find an anxious Turner still on course. But it was 7:30 and

Allahabad was somewhere far behind us. Turner had mistaken distant heat lightning for the Allahabad beacon.

"There was no alternative but to back-track some two hundred miles. We did a 'one-eighty' and prayed that the fuel would hold out. It was night and pitch black. We were over dense jungle and wondered what we ought to do if the engines quit. At first we considered taking to our 'chutes, but the prospect of meeting any one of scores of jungle creatures made taking our chances in a dead-stick landing the better choice. Romping with Roscoe's pet lion was one thing, but a Bengal tiger was something else!

"Reeder Nichols, our radio man, got in touch with Allahabad, but the operator there was so busy broadcasting our misfortune that he didn't have time to give us the proper homing signals. We had a direction finder and if he had continued to give us signals we could have established our position. Finally Turner ordered Nichols to send out an S.O.S. and all broadcasting stopped immediately.

"We then told Allahabad to keep sending to us and thus managed to find our way back to the field. As we taxied up to the gas pits both engines sputtered and quit; that's how close it was! We had wasted more than three hours of flying time!"

The K.L.M. DC-2, which had been ahead of the Boeing, had heard the Americans' distress signals. "I would like to have gotten my fingers around the neck of that fellow in Allahabad," Parmentier later told Pang. "I would have choked him good!"

From Allahabad the Americans headed for Rangoon, flying directly across the Bay of Bengal to save time. They were the only ones to do so, the others electing to follow the safer land route around the bay. The Bay was smooth as glass and the Americans could see their plane's reflection on the mirror-like surface.

Later they received a message that a typhoon was moving in their direction, so they altered course toward Alor Star. The next advisory informed them that the alternate field was a sea of mud. The Boeing was running low on fuel, however, and there was no choice but to land. They found a dry strip at one side of the runaway, refueled, and took off for Singapore.

Stormy weather was encountered all the way to the southern tip of the Malay Peninsula, but fortunately the weather cleared and they sat down on a good field, well lighted with flares. Here they had their third meal of ham and eggs, the only food they dared eat since leaving England. Here, too, they learned that contestants were strung out behind them as far back as Rome. They also learned that the DeHavilland Comet and the Dutchmen in the DC-2 were still in front.

From Singapore the course was plotted to Darwin on Australia's north coast. Head winds, however, forced them to land in the Dutch East Indies for more fuel before heading out over the Timor Sea. The Boeing landed at Kopang and was met by a big Dutchman. The Americans explained who they were and why they had landed, but the Dutchman said he knew nothing of any race, and demanded a $16 landing fee. Turner paid the fee and asked for a ground crew to fuel the Boeing. But there was no help to be had and the Americans had to do their own fueling.

Pangborn's navigating across the Timor Sea brought the Boeing into Darwin dead on course. But by then Scott and Campbell-Black were already in Melbourne. The DC-2 was still ahead, but with luck the Americans might close the gap. Pangborn plotted a course for Charleville by way of the west coast of the Gulf of Carpenteria. This route was roughly a hundred miles longer than the direct line, but offered check points that reduced the likelihood of becoming lost in the thinly populated area of northern Australia.

On this stage Reeder Nichols sent messages that were heard in San Francisco some 7,000 miles away. Earlier in the flight he had talked from Iran to Manila. Both these messages were world records for transmissions from the air to ground stations.

Nearing Charleville, Turner noticed a drop in oil pressure on one engine. On landing they made minor repairs and learned that the Dutchmen were stuck in the mud at Albury, which meant that the Americans had a chance for second place. The Boeing was soon in the air, closing the gap, but again the engine oil pressure began to drop. Again they had no option but to land, this time at Bourke, some five hundred miles from Melbourne.

With nearly 11,000 miles behind them, the Americans were determined to finish the race, and pushed on with the faulty engine. Though the oil pressure became dangerously low, they lucked out and, nose down, zoomed across the finish line to a rousing welcome from 150,000 spectators.

Checking in with the official timers, the Americans found that the Dutchmen had landed just two and one-half hours ahead of them. Had they not lost three hours when Turner over-flew Allahabad, they might have come in second. But the K.L.M. crew had had their problems, too. Lost in a violent thunderstorm at night on the last stage of the race, they had sent out an appeal for a position fix from any town that heard their engines.

The radio operator at Albury heard the Douglas circling, but was unable to make the Dutchmen understand the name of the town. He sent a fellow worker to the local power station to flash the name of the town by blinking the street lights in Morse code. This time they made contact.

The DC-2 landed safely, but was quickly mud-bound. It required two hundred volunteers, plus the full 1,400 horsepower of the twin Cyclones to free the big transport from the Australian gumbo. Parmentier off-loaded his passengers to lighten the load for take-off. Thus the contest between the two most advanced airliners in the world ended inconclusively, both crews having experienced delays on the ground.

The race rules provided that no single team could win prizes in both speed and handicap divisions. The Comet pilots, Scott and Campbell-Black, had already won the speed event. The K.L.M. crew, having finished second, opted for first in the handicap division. Thus, by order of succession, having finished third overall, the Americans became the recipients of second-place money in the speed division.

Australian papers reported that Turner and Pangborn, on their arrival, appeared almost as spruce and fit as the Dutch crew, which stepped from the Douglas in neatly pressed uniforms. The people of Melbourne were disappointed, according to the *New York Times,* because Turner had not been accompanied by Gilmore, his famous pet lion.

The English winners, on the other hand, were near collapse as they climbed from the Comet. "We had a lousy trip and that's praising it," Scott declared as he headed straight for bed. The winning time was 70 hours 59 minutes which worked out to an unexciting 159.1 m.p.h. The Comet, theoretically capable of 230 m.p.h., had suffered engine troubles along with everyone else.

Tragedy struck early in the race, resulting in the death of two Englishmen, Flying Officer H.D. Gilman and J.Y.C. Baines, his co-pilot. Their British Fairey Fox, one of two in the race and the only military aircraft to start, crashed shortly after it had taken off from Rome. For a time it was feared that two Americans, Jack Wright and John Polando, were lost. After a night of anxiety, word came from Basra, Iraq, that they had been forced down in Persia. The authorities, ignorant of the great race in progress, had thrown the New Yorkers in jail. They remained incarcerated for twelve hours, which put their speedy Monocoupe hopelessly out of the race.

Turner and Pangborn received $7,500 as their share of the prize money. The Boeing 247D was handed over to United Air Lines, where it served faithfully for a number of years, and the fliers went their separate ways.

27

Swana

WITH NO MAJOR undertakings in prospect, but holding firm to his devotion to the air, Pang tested and demonstrated various types of aircraft in the years from 1935 to 1940. He worked several years for Burnelli, Bellanca, and Cunliffe-Owen Aircraft of Southampton, England, who were building Burnelli planes under license. He conducted official tests of the aircraft in company with Royal Air Force test crews at Martlesham Heath and Boscombe Down. He was the first foreigner to be licensed as an official test pilot in England.

His finances improved. He was finding that a much smaller gross resulted in a much higher net when he operated alone, contrasted to the long-time joint operation with Van Gates. In New York he made his headquarters at the Lexington, like so many of the aviation crowd, and stayed at equally posh hotels in Canada and England, and came to know some of the better restaurants in New York and London.

Romance had never played much of a role in Pangborn's life. He had expressed it succinctly when he had first experienced heart flutter in California, and the girl's mother had offered a ranch as a wedding present.

"What a chance!" Pang said, "But there was the sky, prairies, and mountains. I didn't want a tomorrow of security and serenity. I was in the middle of a world that jumped into life and bloom every morning. So I said to myself: 'let's get the hell out of here!' "

In New York Pang had received a letter from Fritz, the girl he'd met at Tokyo. She wrote: "Evans brought down some of the things you left at Sabishiro and he will pick up the others at Tachikawa

John W. Underwood photo collection.

The Burnelli UB-14B.

airport. The morning after we returned to Tokyo I was besieged by reporters and photographers. Somehow or other the rumor had circulated that I was engaged to you and would be leaving for America shortly. Of course I denied it all, but it was pretty difficult because . . . well, I'm very fond of you. By the way, I hope the chow wasn't too terrible. My intentions were good anyway."

Later Fritz wrote about rumors that he was engaged to a Miss "Proats." No doubt she was referring to a Miss Coates in California who, on conclusion of the Pacific flight, had said in an interview, "Yes, Pang and I are engaged in a way. And am I thrilled. I think the flight was wonderful." But nowhere does Pang mention such an involvement.

Then, on vacation in the Alps in 1939, Pang assisted a fallen skier from a snowdrift. She was Swana Beaucaire Duval, a French actress of beauty and charm. They were married a few months later.

With the Allies at war with Germany, England was looking to the United States for arms, particularly aircraft. Canadian factories, too, were turning out planes for the war effort. At first the American and Canadian aircraft were delivered by ship, with resulting slowness and staggering losses due to submarine activity.

Prime Minister Winston Churchill proposed to President Roosevelt that the planes be flown across the Atlantic. Pangborn was asked to assist in recruiting a Ferry Command unit of the Royal Air Force. He was named senior captain of the command.

Leaving his bride in New York, Pang set out on a whirlwind tour of the United States recruiting scores of pilots. They were either to be flight instructors in England or to ferry aircraft across the ocean. Training facilities were set up at Dorval, Quebec. After the war the "Dorval Survivors," with Pang as first president, was formed by those who had gone through the Canadian facility.

As senior captain of the Command, Pangborn made 170 crossings of the Atlantic and Pacific. Among the aircraft he ferried were PBYs, Lockheed Hudsons, Douglas C-47s, Liberators, Lancasters, Boeing B-17 Flying Fortresses, Douglas DC-4s, Martin B-26s, North American B-25s, and Mosquito bombers. On several flights delivering PBYs, Bernt Balchen, whom Pang had recruited into the Command, was his navigator.

On one such delivery to Manila Balchen's amazing navigation abilities were demonstrated. Leaving Pearl Harbor, he navigated unerringly to Midway. On the next leg to tiny Wake Island, Pang expressed some misgivings.

"Don't worry, we can't miss it," Balchen said.

They flew on hour after hour. Pang became apprehensive. From his navigation table, and without looking outside the plane, the Norseman finally spoke, "Be there in two minutes."

Pang continued for one and three-quarter minutes, and then burst out, "Godamnit, Bernt, there isn't a thing ahead but ocean."

"Look below," Bernt said.

There, directly below them was the tiny,white-ringed atoll.

These frequent and protracted absences on flights to distant overseas points, compounded by Pang's disdain for the humdrum of city life, put a strain on the marriage.

In August, 1940, the *Oakland Tribune* carried a story worthy of the best of the sob-sisters. It reported that Swana had come to Reno to get a divorce. Her grounds were incompatibility and the fact that Pang's duties in the Ferry Command kept him away too much. Then, according to the newspaper, she had gone to a movie—a "tear-jerker" about the unhappiness of divorce—and had been so touched

The beautiful French actress Swana Beaucaire Duval, whom Pangborn rescued from a ski-slope spill and later married. Although they were later divorced, they remained friends.

emotionally that she had wired Pang asking him to join her in Reno for a reconciliation. "I was divorcing him because his flying kept him away from me. Now he can fly and I'll stick with him," she was quoted.

Apparently the effects of the Reno movie quickly wore off,

because Swana returned to New York and reinstated action for the divorce. After considerable litigation she won a decree and a monthly monetary settlement.

Following the divorce, a long time friend, William Loeb, New Hampshire publisher of the *Manchester Union Leader*, wrote Pang: "I was sorry to hear about the divorce, but to expect you and Swana to get along would be as unnatural as to mix water and oil. I often think of the evening that Swana and you and I were at the Versailles. New York's sophisticated life was her life, whereas you and I had an entirely different approach to life."

Following the war, and still rejecting all suggestions by his brother that he come west and settle down, Pang pursued the routine of earning a living in the only way he knew, or cared about. Despite his thousands of hours in the air, he was considered too old by the airlines. It is doubtful if he could have adjusted to the routine of flying the same route over and over again, or observed the rigid procedures of the airlines.

Instead, he ferried civilian aircraft across the Atlantic and engaged in a variety of flying activities in the United States and Mexico. He considered a proposal to use a modified Lockheed P-38 in an attempt to break Bill Odum's around-the-world speed record. In 1950, he entered into negotiations with Aerographic Surveys Corporation concerning aerial mapping of Angola and Mozambique at a quoted price of one dollar per square mile.

As he neared his sixtieth birthday Pang was feeling the effects of the years in open cockpits in all kinds of weather, the greasy hamburgers consumed hastily in airport cafes, and the brutal pounding he had taken in the crash in Colorado. It was all catching up with him. Taking off in a PBY from San Diego on a ferry flight to Tahiti he found it difficult to get the control column back, and complained that the strain had given him severe pains in his chest and upper arm. Unknown to Pangborn, he had suffered a mild heart attack.

In the fall of 1957 he suffered another attack, this time of major consequence. He was rushed to the hospital in New York and remained there for nearly six weeks. When he was able to travel, his good friend, Frank Ambrose, invited him to come to Florida to recuperate. Ambrose, a former member of the flying circus, had become a millionaire dealing in used aircraft.

News of Pang's illness spread throughout aviation circles. Colonel Robbins, in Geneva, received a letter. It read: "Just heard about Clyde's illness. Please let me know how he is and where he is." It was signed "Swana." Although they were divorced, the French beauty apparently still felt warmth for the man who preferred the freedom of the skies to married life.

Meanwhile, in New York, Pang's scores of friends, aware of his long illness and strained finances, were arranging a benefit dinner which they scheduled for March 20, 1958. Ambrose, knowing Pang was in a very poor condition, tried to dissuade him from attending the affair. When Pang persisted, Ambrose insisted on going along.

As they arrived in New York a severe storm was raging. Pang caught cold and, completely exhausted, had to remain in his room while nearby six hundred friends gathered to honor him at the dinner in the Lexington hotel. A substantial check was presented to him.

When the cold and exhaustion continued he was taken to the Veteran's hospital. The cold developed into pneumonia. Pang died on March 29, 1958.

Following memorial services in New York, arranged by the American Legion, Clyde E. Pangborn was buried in Arlington National Cemetary with full military honors.

Thus, at 62, Pang's odyssey came to an end. The odyssey of a country boy from the Idaho panhandle who looked beyond the pines of the Bitter Root mountains to the clear blue sky and saw his future, a future as free as the great-winged birds soaring on air currents swirling around the mountain peaks.

On the sands of Sabishiro Beach in Japan a beautiful wooden shaft marks the take-off point of what was the climax of Pangborn's career. And high on a bluff above the Columbia River at Wenatchee, Washington stands a monolith of granite. It is from the ageless walls of the Grand Coulee. It marks the spot where Pangborn landed his wheelless plane at the end of that phenomenal trans-Pacific flight.

The Pangborn memorial at Wenatchee, Washington. This picture was taken in 1968 during dedication ceremonies. At the base, left, is the author who, as a newspaper reporter, covered the landing. At right, with his wife, is Governor Shunkichi Takeuchi of Japan's Aomori Prefecture. As a young newspaper reporter in 1931, Takeuchi covered the take-off from Sabishiro beach.

Organizations

Clyde E. Pangborn was an active or honorary member of the following organizations:

Adventurers Club of New York
Aero Club of Cannes, France
Air Force Association
American Legion, Wenatchee, Washington
Circumnavigators Club of New York
Circus Saints and Sinners, New York
Elks, Wenatchee, Washington
Explorers Club of New York
Federation Aeronautique International (Gold Medal)
Fellow American Academy of Air Law
Fellow of American Geographic Society
French Foreign Legion V.L.E. (Honorary)
International Police Chiefs Association
Kiwanis, Wenatchee, Washington
League Internationale des Aviateurs
Lions, Wenatchee, Washington
National Aeronautic Association
National Geographic Society
OX5 Club, New York
Quiet Birdmen, New York Hangar
R.A.A.S. Australia (Honorary)
Rotary International, Wenatchee, Washington

Royal Aero Club, London
Royal Air Forces Association
Veteran Pilots Association
Wings Club, New York

AWARDS AND HONORS:

Harmon Trophy, 1931
The Kings Medal (England)
White Medal of Merit (Japan)

Index

AIRCRAFT INDEX

GENERAL INDEX *

A

B

*Since Pangborn and Gates are so prominent a part of this book, listing of the individual pages on which their names occur is not included.

C

N

O

P

T

U

V

W

XYZ